What a terrific book! Twice in 1 Corinthians 7 the apostle Paul urges us to remain in the vocation to which God has called us. I've often paraphrased that by saying "Bloom where you're planted!" I believe that a carpenter, an accountant or a president is just as much a minister as a TV evangelist and that his life and business practice are his most effective sermon. My thanks to Ed Silvoso.

PAT BOONE
ENTERTAINER
LOS ANGELES, CALIFORNIA

Ed Silvoso is the only one who could write this book. His years of laboring both with churches and business leaders have allowed him to catch the heart of one of God's most underused resources: the empowered businessperson. Ed lays out the heritage of God, using businesspeople to accomplish His purposes on Earth. He also challenges the Church, as well as business leaders, to discover the call of God on their lives and to get in the game. This is a must-read for business and church leaders to equip them in partnering together as God intended.

DENNIS J. DOYLE
CEO, WELSH COMPANIES
PRESIDENT, NEHEMIAH PARTNERS
MINNEAPOLIS, MINNESOTA

Anointed for Business is in my top five books on taking faith into the workplace. Ed provides many fresh insights and applications not expressed in other faith-at-work resources. I found it biblically sound with many practical applications. Every Christian in the workplace should read *Anointed for Business*.

OS HILLMAN
PRESIDENT, MARKETPLACE LEADERS AND INTERNATIONAL
COALITION OF WORKPLACE MINISTRIES
AUTHOR, *THE 9 TO 5 WINDOW*

If more Christians realized they were anointed for business, God's kingdom would come much faster to this Earth. Ed Silvoso offers a new and insightful look into the business acumen of our early Christian leaders and how relevant it is for today.

LAURIE BETH JONES
AUTHOR, *JESUS, CEO*; *THE PATH*; *JESUS, INC.*; AND *TEACH YOUR TEAM TO FISH*

Anointed for Business is a welcome addition to the teaching ministry of Ed Silvoso. While his early books have greatly blessed the Body of Christ, this one is destined to release even more of God's ministers into the fulfillment of their destiny. I have been privileged to watch this message become formed in Ed and released to the Body, and I can say from firsthand experience, "Get ready to be blessed!"

RICH MARSHALL
AUTHOR, *GOD@WORK*

Ed Silvoso has once again put his finger on the pulse of God's direction for the Church at this hour. *Anointed for Business* is a revelation that could liberate the Body of Christ and uncover the much-needed resources to finance this last-day move of God. Christians in the marketplace is not a new phenomenon: Luke 19:13 says we should "occupy until He comes." "Occupy" means to "barter, trade, to literally do the work of a banker." God has anointed people in the Body of Christ to be successful in the marketplace. This book will help you discover if you're one of them.

BISHOP VAUGHN MCLAUGHLIN
THE POTTER'S HOUSE
JACKSONVILLE, FLORIDA

Ever wonder if you can make a difference in your community? From pulpits to corporate boardrooms, men and women of God are impacting our society with integrity and righteousness. Each one has been called to be a minister and a witness for Christ—in the home, on the job or at school. Wherever the Lord sends us, we are commissioned as His ambassadors. Ed Silvoso clearly shares principles and practices of marketplace evangelism. He exposes misconceptions and exhorts each of us to be that example for Christ wherever we are. How does that translate into your life? As you read brother Ed's book, you'll have a clearer understanding of the plan and purpose God has for you. Using examples of business professionals and ministers alike, brother Ed expands our perspective on how the Lord desires to use each of us to influence society. As always, he challenges our paradigms of thinking. Ed Silvoso has been raised up to present this message for this hour—for you, for this nation and for the nations of the world.

DR. J. DOUG STRINGER
FOUNDER, SOMEBODY CARES AMERICA
HOUSTON, TEXAS

I believe that societal transformation is high on God's agenda for this generation and that the chief catalytic force to bring it about will be Christian believers ministering in the marketplace. In *Anointed for Business*, Ed Silvoso shows more clearly than anyone else to date exactly how you and I can help make this happen. This is truly a book for the times!

C. PETER WAGNER
CHANCELLOR, WAGNER LEADERSHIP INSTITUTE
COLORADO SPRINGS, COLORADO

Ed Silvoso takes away the myths capturing the minds of many Christians concerning believers in the workplace. I love the way he utilizes familiar Scriptures to bring to life biblical characters who were in the workplace and used mightily by God. The Church must activate and mobilize all believers—including those who are in the workplace—if we are going to see revival. *Anointed for Business* is a timely book. It is a much-needed tool to propel the Church into the harvest. Today's harvest is waiting to be reached in places of business, government and education. I highly recommend this book to every believer.

BARBARA WENTROBLE
AUTHOR, *GOD'S PURPOSE FOR YOUR LIFE*
PRESIDENT, WENTROBLE CHRISTIAN MINISTRIES
DALLAS, TEXAS

Ed Silvoso's clear-cut message could be the catalyst that propels America into a first-century-type revival. *Anointed for Business* is a must-read book for Christians who take the Great Commission seriously.

ZIG ZIGLAR
AUTHOR, *SEE YOU AT THE TOP; 5 STEPS TO SUCCESSFUL SELLING*

ED SILVOSO

ANOINTED
FOR
BUSINESS

Regal

From Gospel Light
Ventura, California, U.S.A.

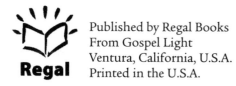

Published by Regal Books
From Gospel Light
Ventura, California, U.S.A.
Printed in the U.S.A.

Regal Books is a ministry of Gospel Light, a Christian publisher dedicated to serving the local church. We believe God's vision for Gospel Light is to provide church leaders with biblical, user-friendly materials that will help them evangelize, disciple and minister to children, youth and families.

It is our prayer that this Regal book will help you discover biblical truth for your own life and help you meet the needs of others. May God richly bless you.

For a free catalog of resources from Regal Books/Gospel Light, please call your Christian supplier or contact us at 1-800-4-GOSPEL or www.regalbooks.com.

First Edition, 2002
Second Edition, 2006

Library of Congress Cataloging-in-Publication Data
The Library of Congress has cataloged the first edition as follows:
Silvoso, Ed.
    Anointed for business / Ed Silvoso.
        p. cm.
Includes bibliographical references.
    ISBN 0-8307-4196-8 (hardcover), 0-8307-4269-7 (trade paperback)
    1. Evangelistic work. 2. Business—Religious aspects—Christianity.
    I. Title.
    BV3793 .S464 2002
    248.8'8—dc21   2002001443

1   2   3   4   5   6   7   8   9   10   /   10   09   08   07   06

Rights for publishing this book in other languages are contracted by Gospel Light Worldwide, the international nonprofit ministry of Gospel Light. Gospel Light Worldwide also provides publishing and technical assistance to international publishers dedicated to producing Sunday School and Vacation Bible School curricula and books in the languages of the world. For additional information, visit www.gospellightworldwide.org; write to Gospel Light Worldwide, P.O. Box 3875, Ventura, CA 93006; or send an e-mail to info@gospellightworldwide.org.

DEDICATION

I dedicate this book to an extraordinary architect of biblical dialogue. He is a person who has a unique ability to build forums broad enough for heterogeneous groups to exchange ideas and thoughts about difficult and controversial issues that directly affect the fulfillment of the Great Commission. He is someone who I have never heard utter a word of criticism directed at those who do not understand what he does or who vehemently disagree with his conclusions. I dedicate this book to C. Peter Wagner, with deep admiration for his character and great gratitude for his impact on the lives of millions, including my own.

CONTENTS

FOREWORD

One of the young students on the campus of a small Christian college took me aside and asked, "Could you come and speak a word of encouragement to those of us in the business college? We are constantly being told by our fellow classmates that unless we go into the ministry, we are just being greedy and not serving the Lord."

I eagerly met with the business college students for more than an hour, sharing what I had seen and heard in the years since my first book, *Jesus, CEO,* was released. I told them of praying with CEOs who were wrestling with how to balance profit and the needs of the people they led. I spoke of businesses leading the charge for social justice in many underdeveloped countries. I shared with the students stories about myriad businessmen and women who were out in the world at large, making a difference in huge ways—none of whom were using a pulpit to do so. In fact, I smiled when I shared that to my knowledge, Jesus only spoke from a pulpit one time, and that was when He was still a child.

Ed Silvoso has put into words so many of these truths—truths that I hold dear: that the field that is truly ripe for harvest is not in the churches, but in the boardrooms; not at the baptistery fonts, but by the water coolers; not in the pews, but in the cubicles.

My great passion is to have every person recognize and serve the Lord with his or her highest gift. Existing hierarchies in the Church lead to a very narrow and often lonely place for leadership and influence. There can only be a few pastors serving hundreds or thousands of people.

Yet the business world offers less of a stained-glass ceiling for any person, regardless of gender, color, education or training, than almost any other area of service. The business world says, "If you have an idea, service, or goods that serve others, we want it, and we don't care what color you are, how old you are, whether you wear skirts or pants, or have a degree on your wall." No matter who we are, we can bring our gifts to the marketplace so they can be multiplied.

Jesus spoke very strong words about the implicit responsibility on each of us to take the talents we have been given and to multiply them.

For those who know that they are destined for business, love it without explanation or cause, or can't seem to stop thinking of ways to come up with better ideas, goods, services or processes, the marketplace provides a very rewarding and fulfilling path. Actually, as Ed Silvoso writes, for large numbers of us, the business world is our place of ministry.

I once counseled a preacher who was weeping almost uncontrollably. He admitted to me that he had never wanted to be a pastor, but that his mother had dedicated him on the altar soon after his birth and never let him forget it.

When I asked him what he really wanted to do, if all things were possible, he dried his tears on his robe and said, "I would love to be a baker." His face lit up like a Christmas tree at the very thought of it. I smiled and said, "Then go do that." He hesitated for a moment, and then said, "Would you mind calling my wife?" This is a man destined to make a lot of dough, you might say, and I am certain that the Body of Christ would benefit far more from a happy baker who is transforming the world from his place in the marketplace than a miserable preacher trying to get through his next appearance in the pulpit.

What my friend Ed Silvoso has done, and continues to do, is to throw open the doors and set people free. No longer do Christians need to be bound by false guilt that says making money is evil or wrong; that poverty is noble; that only those with preacher or pastor, reverend or saint before their name can fully please God.

Ed Silvoso gives us countless examples from real life and Scripture that remind us that the Bible was full of spiritreneurs, and that especially today many among us are indeed anointed for business.

If you picked up this book, then perhaps you are one of those called to make a difference in the marketplace. I will rejoice when I hear the words spoken over you, "Well done, good and faithful servant." It is those words I most desire to hear as I labor in my various businesses, and I know it is those words that motivate Ed Silvoso as well.

Read on, and be blessed.

Laurie Beth Jones
Author of *Jesus, CEO; The Path;* and
The Four Elements of Success

ANOINTED
FOR
BUSINESS

INTRODUCTION

The marketplace—the combination of business, education and government—is to a metropolis what the heart is to the human body. Through these three arteries flows the life of a city. A city cannot exist without a marketplace in the same fashion that a body cannot live without a heart.

Some of my earliest memories are of the marketplace.

I grew up in a two-story house overlooking the main plaza in San Nicolas, Argentina.[1] Like in every Spanish town, the plaza was the center of life. The Plaza Hotel, flanked by the Catholic cathedral and the police station, was on our block. On the east side were the courthouse, the National College and the Social Club, where the city fathers gathered. On the north side were Customs, the Italian Club and homes of the leading lawyers and politicians. On the west side were the National Bank, more homes and a popular restaurant that between meals set tables on the sidewalk and doubled as the town café. City Hall was three blocks away, but it made its presence felt by the sonorous carillon that faithfully announced the time at 15-minute intervals 24 hours a day.

The plaza was wedged between the port and the city's two main streets where most of the businesses operated. It was such a vital part of the city that everything of substance happened in or around it. It was there that the military parades and political rallies took place. On Saturday evenings beautiful girls and handsome boys would choreograph the ritual of courtship under the attentive eyes of mothers, who would stand nearby, and fathers, who would sit at the café and pretend to discuss sports and politics. This area of town was called *el centro* (the center) because everything revolved around it. In essence, it was the marketplace in a microcosm. Through the ages, cultures around the world have fashioned their own versions of the marketplace, but they always included these three basic components that were found around the plaza in my hometown: business, education and government.

THE MARKETPLACE AND
THE EARLY CHURCH

Early Christians made the marketplace the focal point of their ministry because their occupations regularly took them there. As they conducted business, it was natural for them to present the gospel to the people they encountered. Marketplace people played a vital role in the emergence, establishment and expansion of the Early Church—in fact, most of Jesus' followers remained in full-time business while simultaneously conducting full-time ministry. This was possible because they saw the marketplace as their parish and their business as a pulpit. To them witnessing was not an occasional activity but a lifestyle.

The book of Acts unfolds the story of believers who did more than tell people about Jesus in the marketplace. They also witnessed a steady stream of signs and wonders. In fact, only one of the 40 extraordinary manifestations of God's power recorded in Acts happened in a religious venue: the healing of the lame man at the temple gate called Beautiful (see Acts 3:1-11). Most of these spiritual wonders were facilitated by people such as Paul, Priscilla and Aquila, who as ministry *and* business partners are classic examples of marketplace Christians (see Acts 18:1-3).

Generals, not Privates

Today millions of men and women are similarly called to full-time ministry in business, education and government—the marketplace. These men and women work as stockbrokers, lawyers, entrepreneurs, farmers, chief operating officers, news reporters, teachers, police officers, plumbers, factory foremen, receptionists, cooks and much more. Some of them have great influence on mainstream society, others are unsung heroes with low profiles, but each of them has been divinely called to bring the kingdom of God to the heart of the city.

Unfortunately many of these marketplace Christians feel like second-class citizens when compared to people who serve full-time in a church or missionary context. This should not be the case. No matter the occupation, Christians who work at secular jobs need to know that they are not perpetual privates in God's army just because they have not gone to seminary. They need to discover that they have the potential to become full-fledged generals whose ministry is in the heart of the city, instead of inside a religious building.

It is imperative that they realize that not only is it *OK* to do ministry in the marketplace, but that God has explicitly *called* them and *anointed* them for it. By "anointed" I mean that they have been chosen and empowered by the Holy Spirit for a divinely sanctioned assignment. By "ministry" I mean that they can do more than just witness; they can bring transformation to their jobs and then to their cities—as happened in the first century.

Most marketplace Christians already know that their ministry and their occupation are somehow connected, but they do not comprehend exactly how. Even though they sense that they have a call to ministry, they hesitate about exchanging their secular setting for a religious one. Quite often they are told that this vacillation is due to lack of faith or, worse yet, an attachment to worldly things. This indictment leaves them confused because deep down they feel that their spiritual destiny is in the marketplace.

Welcome to the Club!

Unfortunately many of these marketplace ministers fail to fulfill their divine destiny because they are often derided as untrained or uneducated. This is not a new accusation. Peter and John would say, "Welcome to the Club!" In the account we find in Acts, this is exactly what businessmen-turned-ministers were called by the religious clique. This should never happen because the requirement to be a minister is not religious education; rather, it is the spiritual conditioning that comes from "having been with Jesus" (Acts 4:13).

Jerusalem Transformed

It was such conditioning that allowed the apostles to fill Jerusalem with the good news in just a few weeks by leading thousands to the Lord (see Acts 5:28; 6:7). As a result, Jerusalem experienced transformation at the deepest level: The needs of the poor and the widows, two very vulnerable groups, were met (see Acts 6:1-7). The hungry were fed and the sick were healed (see Acts 2:45; 3:8). The gospel even had a positive influence on the Sanhedrin, the most powerful forum the Jews had (see Acts 5:33-39). Solomon's Portico became the place for a steady stream of signs and wonders, giving the emerging Church favor with the people (see Acts 5:12-15). The movement was so dynamic that eventually the streets and sidewalks of Jerusalem were turned into evangelistic venues where sick people lined up hoping that the healing shadow of Peter would fall upon them (see Acts 5:15). Soon multitudes from nearby cities flooded Jerusalem (see Acts 5:16).

What a change! This was the city that had previously grieved Jesus to the point of tears but was now giving Him tremendous joy (see Luke 19:41-42)! It began on the Day of Pentecost when the disciples left the enclosed confines of the Upper Room and went to the open space of the marketplace. On that day Peter, the fisherman, became the first fisher of men, setting a pattern soon to be replicated throughout the Roman Empire. This movement was led not by individuals notorious for their religious acumen, but by people known for their roles in the market-place: fishermen, tax collectors, farmers and more.

Three Business Partners

It did not take too long for these enthusiastic preachers to transform myr-iad towns and cities, culminating with Ephesus, site of the most dramatic power encounter recorded in Acts (see Acts 19:1-13). This city, with a demon-driven economy and a marketplace that was the citadel of evil, expe-rienced a radical transformation. It is not a coincidence that at the center of God's move were Paul, Aquila and Priscilla. Their dual ministry/business status connected them to the religious community through their teachings and to the marketplace by their tent-making enterprise.

Jesus' Recruiting Grounds

Jesus, a recognized craftsman, found the marketplace to be familiar ter-ritory (see Mark 6:3). He recruited His disciples there, not in the Temple. None of the Twelve was a member of the professional clergy or a leader in the synagogue. Paul, who joined the group later and was a rabbi (see Acts 9:1-16), was not a stranger to the marketplace. In fact, on many of his ministry trips, he also ran a profitable business. In Ephesus his for-profit operation was large enough to provide for him, his team and even the needy (see Acts 20:33-35).

The elders of emerging churches often were marketplace leaders who had experienced dramatic conversions—for example, Dorcas, Lydia and Cornelius. Due to their prominence in their cities, they, in turn, produced salvation movements (see Acts 9:36-43; 10:1).

More Than a Layman

Today, in general, religious leaders have little interaction with unbelievers, even less with prominent ones. The Church does not command the attention or the respect of the marketplace. In fact, quite often it is considered irrelevant and seen as some sort of social parasite. To compound this misconception, Church members who do have relevance in the city on account of their position in the marketplace tend to disqualify themselves from leadership in spiritual matters. The most common self-inflicted put-down is "I am not a pastor—I am just a layperson." This is all part of a clever satanic scheme to neutralize apostles, prophets, evangelists, pastors and teachers along with the entire army of disciples, *already* positioned *in* the marketplace.

God calls some people to serve inside the Church, and this is a precious call. Pastors and full-time ministers are the modern equivalent of the Old Testament priests who ministered in the Temple. They clearly play a vital role in spiritual leadership, since they are the ones who, through their examples and Bible-centered teachings, equip the saints for the work of the ministry. Their God-given role cannot be overemphasized—it is crucial. We would not be the Church without them.

With this in mind, we need to see that there are others who are anointed to minister in the marketplace, like the kings, officials and other functionaries who were the contemporaries of the Old Testament priests. The call to serve in the marketplace and the call to serve in traditional religious settings are both *valid* and *interdependent*, since they involve ministers who respond to the same divine calling. Whether people are priests in the Temple or kings in society, God has called each one of them. Unfortunately the former has been exalted to the detriment of the latter. It is about time that people who are called to serve in the marketplace be validated as full-fledged ministers because the last revival, the one predicted by Joel and quoted by Peter (see Acts 2:17-21), will happen all over the city, not just inside a building. It will be an outpouring of the Spirit of God upon *all* flesh.

Spiritual Warfare in the Boardroom

As ministers of God, marketplace Christians need to know that spiritual warfare is a central component of their daily routines, whether they are aware of it or not. Satan and his evil forces constantly try to destroy lives and enterprises in the Church *but even more so in the marketplace.* The extraordinary opposition Christians experience when putting deals together in a godly way is no different from what pastors face when counseling people who are contemplating suicide or divorce. Since Satan is the source of both challenges, the solution is the same: servants willing to turn the spiritual tide by ministering in the power of the Holy Spirit and setting free people who are oppressed by the devil. The location is ancillary.

When marketplace Christians are reduced to second-class status, the Church is automatically deprived of its most strategically placed soldiers because they are the ones closest to Satan's command and control centers. If properly equipped, they can do lethal damage to the systems by which the devil holds people captive in our cities (see 2 Cor. 4:4; Eph. 6:12). This is why he allocates so many of his resources to make marketplace Christians feel unqualified and inferior in spiritual matters.

Four Lethal Misbeliefs

The combination of four major misbeliefs usually neutralizes God's calling on those anointed for marketplace ministry:

1. There is a God-ordained division between clergy and laity.
2. The Church is called to operate primarily inside a building often referred to as the temple.

3. People involved in business cannot be as spiritual as those serving in traditional Church ministry.
4. The primary role of marketplace Christians is to make money to support the vision of those "in the ministry."

I have written this book to expose these unbiblical misbeliefs and to show, from the Scriptures and from history, the central role of Christians in the marketplace. While it is true that in Old Testament days there was a division between the clergy and the laity and that most religious activities took place at the temple, Jesus' New Covenant abolished the old order. In fact, the temple in Acts does not equate with the Church as we know it. The reference to early Christians praying in the temple simply means that they prayed where it was customary. The New Testament replaced the Levitical priestly order with the priesthood of all believers—in other words, every Christian is a minister. That is why today, Church should happen all over the city, every day, all day long as Christians replicate the model presented in Acts 2:42, "They were continually devoting themselves to the apostles' teaching and to fellowship, to the breaking of bread and to prayer."

Nowadays there are multitudes of believers in the marketplace who hold strategic positions in business, education and politics. They need to know that they are called to play a vital part in the establishment of God's kingdom on Earth. Without their active participation *and leadership*, our cities will not be transformed and the Great Commission will not be fulfilled in our generation.

Getting out of the Bleachers

Too often ministry in the Church resembles a final match in soccer's World Cup that has gone into overtime: A handful of players, all in desperate need of rest, run all over the field while hundreds of thousands of spectators, who could use some exercise, watch from comfortable seats. The players are the ministers who exert most of the energy, and the spectators represent the laypeople whose participation is limited to a secondary role, mainly making the whole enterprise financially feasible.

This unbiblical classification of believers results in first- and second-class statuses within the Church. Such distinctions should not exist because Jesus Himself was not an elitist. Even though He recruited 12 apostles and appointed them to positions of leadership, He was always inclusive. When He spoke, except when He addressed specific situations pertaining to the Twelve, He invariably spoke *to* and *for* everybody. If we are to fulfill the Great Commission, we must follow Jesus' lead and eliminate class division.

No one is better placed in the city than Christians who operate in the marketplace. God has already given them jurisdiction in businesses, schools and government circles. The promise that "every place on which the sole of your foot treads, I have given it to you" (Josh. 1:3) applies to them also—and they tread all over the city on a daily basis! The Lord is in their hearts. The Holy Spirit is imbuing their spirits. The Word is planted in their minds. All they need now is to realize that they are anointed to minister in the fullness of the Spirit. When this happens, they will be able to push back the spiritual darkness that envelops our cities. As marketplace Christians begin to move in their anointing, the whole world will hear the voice of God. This is what this book is about!

Note
1. San Nicolas, Argentina, has a population of 130,000.

CONFESSIONS OF A CHRISTIAN BUSINESSMAN

"One day you will be the president of Argentina!" my grandpa announced for the umpteenth time. My uncles and aunts endorsed his prediction with enthusiastic applause and cheers.

Born and raised in Argentina, I am the first male child in an Italian-Spanish family. I have only one sibling—a sister—and my cousins on the Italian side are my juniors by 10 or more years. As the male heir to the family name I was the focus of exuberant affirmation by my grandparents, parents, uncles and aunts. To my elders I was *il bambino di oro,* "the golden boy." Everyone had grandiose dreams for me to fulfill.

Some, led by my grandpa, repeatedly told me that I was destined to be the leader of Argentina. They reminded me that at the moment of my birth the attending physician had declared, "Behold the future president!" My father was in politics, so it seemed natural that I would emulate him. I was accustomed to watching him address crowds and rouse them with his booming voice as he spoke passionately about social issues. He led workers' marches that demanded free elections; elections that, once held, put Juan Peron in power. Subsequently, he worked with Evita Peron to help the poor and to advance civil rights. Raised in such an environment, a political career was not a foreign idea to me. In fact, it was expected.

On the other hand, the religious sector of my family proclaimed that I was destined for the papacy. They told me that even though I would have to start as a priest like everybody else, I should get on the fast track so that I could become the youngest and first Argentine-born pope in history. At the time, I was an altar boy and active in the Catholic Action Movement; thus, this option also fell within the realm of the possible.

> The more I prayed, the more God's hand showed up at work. The more He intervened, the better each project turned out.

Then there were some kinfolk who insisted that I go into business. Someone would add, with a chuckle, "And when you become *very* rich, you can take care of all of us." I had a natural knack for numbers. I did well in school and I was very good at trading *figuritas,* the Argentine equivalent of baseball cards. This resulted in my having a large collection, which in the world of children was synonymous with wealth and success. Watching me wheel and deal, some of my elders predicted that I would surely advance to the major leagues of business and make it big.

At the time I did not know what I would become when I grew up, but I did know that eventually I would take up one of these three careers. Barely in my teens, I became a Christian in a Protestant church and the field was instantly narrowed to one option. Accepting Jesus as my Savior was the best decision of my life; but, it automatically eliminated the possibility of running for president because the Argentine Constitution, at the time, prohibited non-Catholics from rising to the highest political office in the land. Since a Protestant cannot become pope, that option was also gone, leaving me with just one: business.

This is how, in my early 20s, I became the youngest hospital administrator in the region, in charge of a new facility served by 51 doctors. Given my lack of seasoned experience, due to my young age, I was painfully aware that I needed *supernatural* help. Therefore, prayer became the backbone of my business routine. The more I prayed, the more God's hand showed up at work. The more He intervened, the better each project turned out. After watching me successfully fend off a hostile business takeover, many of the doctors entrusted me with the management of their personal finances. We invested in a community bank and I was given a seat on its board. When more money found its way into our portfolio, we set up a lending company. Before long, I was wearing three business hats: hospital administrator, member of the board of a bank and CEO of a lending company.

It was challenging, to say the least. Doing business always brings up the possibility of corruption, even more so in Argentina. Evading taxes, keeping a double set of books and violating labor laws were considered *normal* practices. However, I was unwavering about sticking to the right side of the road. At first my bosses were reluctant because they feared that they would lose the competitive advantage that came from avoiding taxes and taking questionable shortcuts. But as they saw how well we did when deals were done the ethical way, they began to trust me more. Eventually they gave me full freedom to act as I saw fit. As long as we made money, they did not mind my unusual standards.

THE JESUS CHAIR

I thoroughly enjoyed dealing, buying, selling and hiring. The pressure was always on, but each time it approached the boiling point, I reached for what I called the Jesus chair. This was a chair I had purposely placed in my office. When things became unmanageable, I would close the door, kneel by the chair and ask for divine guidance. Repeatedly God provided it. Sometimes He did it in a quiet way. At other times He gave me specific directions. More than once He performed business miracles in answer to those prayers. It was so reassuring to know that Jesus was there and that He had anointed me for the job I had!

In spite of the constant pressure when at work, I felt good about my job. However, when at church, that was not always the case—especially in meetings where the call to the ministry was discussed.

Why? Because some well-meaning but misguided leaders looked down on my occupation. Time and again they would demand, "When are you going to go into the ministry? You don't live by faith but by sight. At work you hang around sinners, people who drink and smoke. You have a calling on your life. Do not be rebellious. Leave everything and go into the ministry."

This criticism from my spiritual leaders was confusing and frustrating.

It was *confusing* because deep down I knew that God was with me at work as much as He was with me in church. I experienced God's presence in both places. At work, my spiritual assignment was to make Christ known. At church I was to learn, worship and lead others into deeper relationships with God. The primary difference was that on the job I depended *exclusively* on works (such as business miracles). By this I mean that in order to fulfill the mission God had given me there, His guidance and supernatural intervention were *essential*. Besides, I could not afford to separate my job from spiritual things. I would not have lasted one day if it had not been for the constant power and presence of God at work.

Another reason I felt compelled to stay on the job was that I was an informal pastor to my business associates. Quite often I found myself in smoke-filled rooms, praying with them, or at a party, ministering to members of their families—*some of them received the Lord!* None of this was short of a miracle considering that most of them were staunch Catholics who were part of a social class far above that of most people in my church. *How could all of this ministry on the job be so bad?* I wondered.

It was *frustrating* because I respected my elders; in my eyes not to follow their leading was tantamount to rebellion. I was also perplexed because when help was needed in matters involving the government, finances or employment, those same leaders did not hesitate to ask for my assistance. *If I were so contaminated, why were my money and my services solicited so often?*

IN MINISTRY AFTER ALL

I have a wonderful wife. Ruth and I have been married for 33 years. We have four children and six grandchildren. When we got married, we acknowledged that our lives and careers were the Lord's and that our highest aspiration was to serve Him fully. Eventually God led me to exchange my business career for church ministry. I vividly remember the day I submitted my resignation. My bosses did not want me to leave and kept pressuring me to name the price that would cause me to reconsider. After successfully turning down a string of very tempting salary-increase offers, Ruth and I left town to take a pastorate where the remuneration was 30 times less. The lower income did not bother us, even though our first child, Karina, had just been born and this meant increased expenses.

We have never regretted taking that step, but in 1999 I unexpectedly came in touch with a very tender spot in my soul. Later in this book I will provide the details of how this came about, but its essence was the discovery that deep down, covered by a wall of human-made shame, lay buried the fact that God had anointed me for business with the same anointing I was so familiar with in church ministry. This discovery led me to understand that the day I tendered my resignation, I did not leave something bad to go into the ministry—I had been a minister all along!

Once my eyes were opened, I was again able to get *guiltlessly* in touch with the joy I had when I was running three businesses. For the first time in more than three decades, it was good to feel no shame or worldliness about it. I felt like the prodigal son being embraced by the father and given new robes.

ANOINTED FOR BUSINESS?

The Holy Spirit has since illuminated Scriptures that clearly teach that there is a divine anointing for business. As a result, many portions of the Word have come to light to show that those called to make the marketplace their parish already have the *fullness* of the Holy Spirit and *all* of His gifts to take the kingdom of God to the heart of the city. In order to do this they are entitled and expected to use these gifts in the same fashion that professional ministers use them when they stand behind a pulpit. Practically, this means doing business in the power of the Holy Spirit and having "church" all over the city, just as the early Christians did (see Acts 2:42). Even though I was not able to express it so clearly in my youth, this was exactly what I used to do in my job because I had been anointed for business!

To be anointed for business is to be set aside by God for service in the marketplace. Once anointed, we are to use our job as a ministry vehicle to transform the marketplace so that the gospel will be preached to, and heard by, every creature in our sphere of influence. The same principle applies in all areas of the marketplace: business, education and government.

Anointing in the Bible

Anointing is an important subject in the Scriptures that is often associated with oil, which symbolizes the Holy Spirit. Pouring, rubbing or smearing something or someone with oil was the biblical way to indicate that a person, item or place had been set aside for divine use (see Gen. 28:18). When a person was anointed, a large amount of oil was poured on the head to symbolize that the totality of the person was set aside. Such an anointing was done for full-time consecration. Kings, priests, prophets and places were set aside *in toto* for divine service. Part-time anointing, or anointing for part-time ministry, *is not found in the Bible*.

In Psalms we are shown the picture of oil running down the head, the beard and eventually the robes of Aaron (see 133:1-3). The passage compares the anointing to the dew of Hermon, which comes down upon the mountains of Zion. Abundant, overflowing, enveloping, transforming anointing is what we see in this psalm.

This level of anointing is precisely what God has in mind for people in the marketplace. He wants to anoint them with so much of His Holy Spirit that they will "open their eyes so that [sinners] will turn from darkness to light and from the dominion of Satan to God" (Acts 26:18). This anointing is meant to transform people *and their environment* "that they may receive forgiveness of sins and an inheritance among those who have been sanctified by faith in [God]" (Acts 26:18).

Gifts in the Marketplace

Jesus' promise that believers will be filled with the Holy Spirit, cast out demons, neutralize lurking threats (serpents), survive evil schemes (surreptitious poisonous drinks) and make sick things well (see Mark 16:17-18) *primarily* applies to ministry in the marketplace.

There are two reasons for this. First, the context for Jesus' words is the command, "Go into *all* the world and preach the gospel to all creation" (Mark 16:15, emphasis added). The process described by Jesus is *definitely* centrifugal and expansive. The entire world, the totality of creation, must be the focus of the mission entrusted to us, not just a church building or a gathering of believers.

Second, only demons with suicidal tendencies would dare hang around Spirit-led, Bible-centered church meetings. Most demons spend the bulk of their time in the command centers that still control unredeemed business, education and government circles in most cities. It is precisely there where God's power is desperately needed. And who is already strategically positioned in those places? Believers who are called to minister in the marketplace!

Strategies That Reach Cities

Since I wrote *That None Should Perish* and *Prayer Evangelism*,[1] the ministry team at Harvest Evangelism (the organization that I lead) has been deeply involved in city-reaching thrusts all over the world. We come alongside pastors to help them motivate, train and mobilize members of their congregations so that every person in their cities will have someone praying for them each day. In the last 10 years we have seen significant progress: A number of prototypes have emerged, and there have been significant breakthroughs in many cities.

Yet these new insights concerning the marketplace have energized city-reaching thrusts like nothing else has. In places where the movement had stalled, bringing businesspeople, educators and government leaders on board has been like adding booster rockets to a sputtering airplane. But the most extraordinary benefit has been the renewal in the lives of Christians in the marketplace. These men and women have always had the desire to do something extraordinary for God, but they have been stopped by the limitations imposed upon them by the old paradigm.

Consequently, when it comes to assessing their roles in the marketplace, they have seen themselves as spiritual prisoners of war, desperately trying to survive with dignity in an evil environment. Because they were taught that the marketplace is off-limits to the fullness of the kingdom of God, they never felt empowered to embrace the possibility of seeing it transformed. The best they dared hope for was to be good witnesses and maybe lead someone to Christ. Thus, the notion that the kingdom of God could materialize in their midst to displace the evil kingdom has lain beyond the outer limits of their expectations. This in turn has forced them to settle for merely living an honorable life in a dishonorable environment.

> **Demons spend their time in the command centers that control unredeemed business, education and government circles.**

A New Paradigm

When the pivotal role of the marketplace in God's plans is unveiled, a new paradigm emerges. Marketplace Christians soon discover that in the same fashion that traditional pastors minister God's transforming power to individuals and to domestic institutions such as marriage and family in the context of the church, they also can minister to the people and secular institutions that operate in the marketplace. All of a sudden the marketplace ceases to be a stronghold of the devil that needs to be avoided, and it becomes a place of dynamic ministry to stage its spiritual transformation.

To better understand this we need to see how Jesus viewed the marketplace and His role in it. We will look at this in the next chapter.

Note
1. *That None Should Perish* and *Prayer Evangelism* are both published by Regal Books, Ventura, California. Excerpts from these books can be accessed at www.harvest evan.org.

JESUS AND THE MARKETPLACE

Matthew quotes a reference to Jesus as the "carpenter's son," using the Greek word *"tekton."* Tekton means "artificer, craftsman." Mark quotes a similar reference, which specifically refers to Jesus as a "carpenter," a tekton. Neither Joseph nor Jesus were simple woodworkers; they were craftsmen, carefully making implements of wood.

TROY HALTOM, *BEARING ONE ANOTHER'S BURDENS*

What was Jesus' view of the marketplace? We tend to see Him as antagonistic toward it because He condemned the Temple merchants and because of His radical suggestion that the wealthy young ruler should give away all of his possessions. Was He really hostile toward business and wealth? Exactly what was His attitude?

Traditionally we picture Jesus as remote, more of a monk than a manager. However, because of the roles He embodied—ruler, teacher and businessman—He belongs in the marketplace even more than in a monastery.

BORN IN THE MARKETPLACE

Jesus was in touch with the marketplace from the very beginning of His life on Earth. He was born in a place of business, the stable of an inn (see Luke 2:7), and the angelic worship service to celebrate His birth took place in a nearby feed lot (see Luke 2:13-14).

Rather than religious leaders, Jesus' first visitors were employees and small-business owners. They were shepherds (see Luke 2:15-20) whom His parents received in the inn's parking lot. I point this out because the stable was the equivalent of the modern service station—it was used to dispense food (fuel) to the mules and donkeys (vehicles) that rested (parked) there for the night.

Each of these events could have happened in the Temple or in its courts. Instead, God sovereignly chose secular venues. I believe this was intended to show God's heart for the marketplace, where sinners, the object of His love, spend much of their time. It also could be that Jesus wanted to get in touch with the heart of the city, the marketplace, from the beginning of His earthly life. As He grew older, He identified even further by becoming a craftsman.

JESUS IN BUSINESS

We easily see Jesus as a teacher by virtue of how well He taught and because in the Gospels He is referred to as a rabbi. We also recognize Him as the ultimate ruler because He is the King of kings. However, picturing Him as a businessman is what we have the most difficulty doing today. Yet in the Gospels the opposite was true. At first Jesus was more recognizable as a businessman than as a rabbi or a ruler.

Shortly after He began to preach, His neighbors in Nazareth asked, "'Is this not the carpenter, the son of Mary, and brother of James, and Joses, and Judas, and Simon? Are not His sisters here with us?' And they took offense at Him" (Mark 6:3). Please notice how Jesus' neighbors described Him by his occupation—the carpenter—but had difficulty seeing Him as a credible teacher, much less as a ruler. Such possibilities caused them to take offense at Him, perhaps because they could not accept a local businessman as credible in spiritual matters.

> It was not difficult for Jesus' neighbors to see Him as a businessman since many may have purchased products made by His hands.

It was not difficult for those neighbors to see Jesus as a businessman since many may have engaged His professional services and purchased products made by His hands. A carpenter, in biblical times, was a builder who primarily used wood. Jesus did not do carpentry work occasionally or in His spare time; rather, just like every boy in Israel He was taught a trade in His teens, perhaps even earlier. This means that by the time of His baptism He had been working at His profession for at least 20 years. He was not a mere apprentice but a well-established artisan.

I suspect that many of His neighbors ate at tables made by Jesus and secured their homes with doors built in His shop. Their houses could have had beams cut and fit by the Savior. Even some of their oxen may have worn *Jesus-made* yokes.

It is interesting to note that Jesus even drew upon His experience as a craftsman when He taught and ministered to the multitudes. He was not simply using a catchy metaphor. When He said, "Take my *yoke* upon you, and learn from me, for I am gentle and humble in heart; and you shall find rest unto your souls. For my *yoke* is easy, and my load is light" (Matt. 11:29-30, emphasis added), He knew exactly what He was talking about.

Jesus the Profitable Entrepreneur

Jesus did not merely do carpentry as a hobby. He had learned a trade in order to make a living, and this required that He run His shop at a profit.

His daily business routine likely included the calculation of the cost of goods and labor, the interplay between supply and demand, the establishment of competitive pricing, the measurement of the potential return on His investment, the estimation of maintenance costs and the replacement of equipment. Even though it may be unusual, even uncomfortable, for us to picture Jesus working to make a living, this is precisely what He did for most of His adult life.

In fact, Jesus was not a small-time carpenter who worked only when He was short on money. Early in His ministry His neighbors described Him as "the carpenter's son" (Matt. 13:55) and "the carpenter" (Mark 6:3). If His father, Joseph, had already passed away, then Jesus, as the firstborn male, would have been running the family-owned business. His brothers would have been junior associates, and His mother and sisters would have played supportive roles. This was not a small shop but one large enough to provide a living for this family of eight or more.

Labor was a central part of Jesus' earthly life. According to Jewish tradition, as a rabbi He had to master a trade and exercise it honestly to support Himself to be able to teach for free. Jesus' instruction to others that "it is more blessed to give than to receive," which was quoted by Paul (see Acts 20:35), indicated that He had the means to acquire goods to be given away since He definitely practiced what He preached.

Jesus the Well-Informed Leader

The picture of an ascetic, hermitlike Jesus does not emerge from the Scriptures; rather, it comes from distorted human traditions. It is true that He spent long hours alone in prayer, but He usually did this at night (see Matt. 14:23; Luke 6:12). During the day He interacted with all sorts of people, and His conversation incorporated a very diverse combination of business topics. He was definitely a very well-informed person and one who acquired information through direct exposure to people and situations.

Jesus the Marketplace Connoisseur

Jesus' parables show that He was thoroughly familiar with the marketplace and its operation. His examples dealt with

- construction (see Matt. 7:24-27),
- wine making (see Luke 5:37-38),
- farming (see Mark 4:2-20),
- treasure hunting (see Matt. 13:44),
- ranching (see Matt. 18:12-14),
- management and labor (see Matt. 20:1-16),
- family-owned businesses (see Matt. 21:28-31),
- hostile takeovers (see Luke 20:9-19),
- return on investments (see Matt. 25:14-30),
- futures markets (see Luke 12:16-21),
- crop yield (see Mark 13:27-32),
- management criteria (see Luke 12:35-48),
- the need for observation and research (see Luke 14:24-35),
- misuse of money, and bankruptcy (see Luke 15:11-16),
- the advantage of leverage (see Luke 16:1-13) and
- venture capital in high-risk situations (see Luke 19:11-27).

Jesus the Performer of Business Miracles

Many of Jesus' miracles took the form of business wonders. He produced a tremendous return on a young boy's investment by turning a few fishes and loaves into a complete meal for thousands of people (see Matt. 14:13). The transformation of water into wine belongs in the same category (see John 2:1-10) and illustrates Jesus' sympathy for those in charge of catering. His instructions leading to two miraculous catches of fish are the modern equivalent of an insightful stockbroker's advice (see Luke 5:1-14; John 21:1-6). Peter and his crew—all professional fishermen—must have sold that catch for a significant profit since it was the only fish in town that day. Furthermore, when tax time came along, Jesus gave Peter a hot tip that enabled him to catch a fish that had a coin in its mouth that was worth enough to cover the tax bill for *both* Jesus and Peter (see Matt. 17:24-27).

A Friend of Poor and Rich Alike

Jesus interacted liberally with poor people, yet He was no stranger to the upper end of society. While He was still a toddler, the Magi visited Him.

These men, wealthy professionals specializing in astronomy, medicine and natural science, presented expensive gifts.

Jesus was often the guest of honor at parties offered by wealthy people (see Luke 11:37; 14:7; 19:5). One rich man, Joseph of Arimathea, provided a deluxe burial place for Jesus, a tomb hewn out of a rock, instead of the ordinary ones dug in the ground (see Matt. 27:57-60). Joseph, along with Gamaliel and Nicodemus, was a member of the Sanhedrin. This influential institution was the modern equivalent of the chamber of commerce, the Elks club and the President's Roundtable all rolled into one. This illustrates a point often missed: Jesus befriended the wealthy as well as the poor (I will cover this more in chapter 5).

Financing Jesus' Work

The notion that Jesus was perpetually broke is not scriptural. A group of wealthy women is reported as funding Jesus' ministry. This is mentioned right after He and the Twelve became itinerant preachers (see Luke 8:1,3). This may have become necessary because itinerant preaching must have taken them away from their regular jobs. Drawing from their private funds, these women contributed to the support of Jesus *and* the Twelve (see Luke 8:2-3). Evidently these were women who had significant wealth. This was extraordinary: They were women, *and* they had private, personal wealth. Given the way women were perceived and treated in Jesus' time, this combination was very unusual. Why would Jesus allow the women to help? It was part of His pattern to reach out to people in the marketplace for support, instead of relying upon the religious system of the day.

Jesus' tunic was seamless, which made it the first-century equivalent of an Armani suit. It is true that His parents gave the poor man's offering when they presented Him in the Temple (see Luke 2:22-24) and that His statement about not having a place to lay down His head could mean that He did not own a house (see Luke 9:58). But He always had adequate resources for His ministry and for the support of those traveling with Him. The fact that Judas, the team treasurer, was able to steal money undetected suggests that there were plenty of funds on hand to provide cover for Judas's pilfering (see John 13:29).

Jesus was not a hermit but one who operated with great comfort in the marketplace and who was known to have done honest work for a living. This is also true of His disciples. The notion that Jesus and His followers extracted themselves from society cannot be sustained from the Scriptures. Jesus, a businessman for more than 20 years, recruited people from the marketplace in order to bring the kingdom of God to sinners everywhere. They led intense and normal lives and not once did they dichotomize labor and spiritual matters.

THE INTERPLAY BETWEEN LABOR AND WORSHIP

The relationship between labor and worship is important because work, in the Bible, is never presented as nonspiritual. In fact, God introduced labor (subduing and ruling over the earth) before worship (see Gen. 1:28). He did not do it because labor was superior to worship; rather, He did it because in the Garden, labor *was* worship. Being stewards over God's creation was the way Adam and Eve communed with God, especially when He came down in the cool of the day to check on their affairs (see Gen. 3:8).

Furthermore, after sin had contaminated the soil, God pointed to labor as the tool to use when dealing with the curse (see Gen. 3:17) that had caused the ground to no longer spontaneously yield fruit. At that moment, physical labor—toiling and the sweat of the brow—became the divinely sanctioned means to extract the now-reluctant fruit.

> The relationship between labor and worship is important. In fact, God introduced labor before worship.

Jesus left no doubt about His mission when He announced that in order to set people free He had come to destroy the devil's empire and its ruinous manifestations in their lives (see Luke 4:18-21). The devil's empire was not an abstract idea but a domain firmly entrenched in society to the point that, directly or indirectly, it controlled everyday life (see Eph. 2:1-3; 6:11-12). To destroy this wicked system, Jesus had to dismantle and replace its worldwide societal structure. This is why His objective was not only revival in the Temple or in the myriad synagogues dotting the Roman Empire and beyond—centers where God-fearing people congregated regularly. It was also to bring salvation to the people most enslaved by sin in pagan societies all over the world.

Jesus' strategy was twofold: first, to redeem humankind—which He did through His atoning death, and then to let the captives know that they had been set free. The latter required the launching of something new: the Church (see Matt. 16:18-19). To recruit leadership for this new entity Jesus reached into the marketplace, instead of the rarified religious circles in Jerusalem. This is why His disciples, the backbone for this divine vehicle designed to change the world, were definitely marketplace people, as we will see in the next chapter.

THE
DISCIPLES
AND THE
MARKETPLACE

Jesus intentionally recruited marketplace people who were not members of the religious establishment because His objective was to create a new social vehicle—the Church, a movement that was meant to be the counterculture, rather than a subculture.

T
he first picture we have of the disciples is in the marketplace where Jesus met them. Peter and Andrew, professional fishermen, were busy casting a net into the sea when Jesus told them to follow Him. Jesus next spotted James and John, partners with their father in a food enterprise—they were mending their nets during a lull in the fishing (see Matt. 4:21-22). Matthew received his calling "while in his tax office" (Matt. 9:9). Nathaniel, whom Jesus saw sitting under a tree, was probably a farmer (see John 1:48). All of the disciples were certainly marketplace people. None of the Twelve was a leader in the Temple or in the synagogue. Bypassing the religious circles was intentional on Jesus' part, as we will soon see.

AUTHORS OF THE WORD

The writing of the Gospels, Christianity's most foundational documents, was entrusted not to religious scholars but to marketplace leaders: a medical doctor (Luke), a retired tax officer (Matthew), a partner in a food enterprise (John) and an unemployed millionaire (Mark).

I point this out about Mark (also called John) because there is evidence to suggest that he came from a wealthy family. His mother, Mary, was the one in whose house many met to pray for Peter's release from prison (see Acts 12:12-17). She must have had a large home to accommodate such a gathering. When Peter knocked at the gate, Rhoda, a maidservant, answered. Poor people did not have servants, and their homes did not have gates. Startled, Rhoda ran inside without opening the gate. Peter kept on knocking but was not heard by the other people inside Mary's house. This indicates that the house must have had a long entranceway.

Maybe it was Mark's comfortable upbringing that caused him to desert Paul and Barnabas in Pamphylia and not go with them to do the work (see Acts 13:13; 15:38). Nevertheless, this wealthy scion was entrusted with the extraordinary privilege of writing one of the Gospels.

THE FIRST CHRISTIANS

The Church was not conceived—in the physiological sense of the word—inside a religious building such as the Temple or a synagogue; rather, it started in the upper room of a private home. The Upper Room—the place where the disciples gathered during the gestation period of the Church—was the spiritual equivalent of the human womb.

What was the Upper Room like?

We usually picture it as no larger than a shack. In musicals and Easter programs it is depicted as a tiny place, about the size of a small hut. But when we stop to think about it, we can see that it must have been a very large place because 120 men and women were *staying* there (see Acts 1:13,15). *Staying* means that they took their meals and slept in it, and it was just one room! It is safe to assume that the Upper Room was possibly the largest chamber in a villa owned by one of the wealthiest men in Jerusalem. The choice of a secular venue for the gestation of the Church must not be overlooked.

> The Church was not conceived inside a religious building; rather, it started in the upper room of a private home.

Comfortable in Nonreligious Settings

Later, when 3,000 converts joined the Church, the apostles did not busy themselves with erecting a religious building—instead they held church all over the city. They did it every day, several times a day (see Acts 2:42). Although they continued to go to the Temple for prayer (see Acts 2:46; 3:1), the bulk of their activities took place in homes where they shared their possessions with those in need and took their meals together with gladness and sincerity of heart while praising the Lord (see Acts 2:44-47).

The fact that Christians in the Early Church complemented their participation in Temple-centered rituals with spontaneous religious activities in homes and on the streets (see Acts 5:12-15) shows how comfortable they were in nontraditional religious settings.

Notable as the Backbone of the Early Church

In addition to the apostles, the human backbone of the Early Church consisted of marketplace leaders such as Lydia, a wealthy wholesaler of expensive fabric who had homes in Philippi and in Thyatira. She was Christ's first European convert. Another of the first believers was Dorcas, a designer and manufacturer of inner garments. She apparently made a good living because she "was abounding with deeds of kindness and charity, which she continually did" (Acts 9:36). The words "abounding" and "continually" imply a high level of giving for which corresponding wealth was required. Dorcas was prominent enough for her death to be brought to the attention of Peter, and her subsequent resurrection to be noticed by an entire town which led many of its citizens to believe in the Lord (see Acts 9:36-42).

Aquila and Priscilla were also businesspeople. They had the same profession as Paul: tent makers (see Acts 18:3). Today the word "tent" evokes images of Boy Scout pup tents, but in the first century most tents were far more elaborate. It is not entirely farfetched to equate a tent maker with a modern-day developer of motels, since tents were used for temporary lodging when a person was away from home. Tent makers also did all kinds of leather work. One of Aquila and Priscilla's largest clients may have been the Roman Army, which had garrisons nearby.

Businesspeople were not the only ones to join the Early Church. Many prominent government officials also became believers. For example, the Ethiopian eunuch was in charge of all the treasure of Candace, queen of Ethiopia (see Acts 8:27). It is most unfortunate that we refer to him by his horrible man-inflicted handicap instead of by his position of influence—he was the finance minister of a prominent kingdom. This shows our discomfort with the marketplace in general and with prominent people in particular. It is likely that when he arrived in Ethiopia, it was not his degrading physical scars but his government position that enabled him to present the gospel to others, mostly people of influence.

There were other prominent people in the Early Church, too. Erastus, the city treasurer (see Rom. 16:23) was a member and Luke addresses Acts to Theophilus, who was most likely a high-ranking government official (see Acts 1:1).[1]

Capable of Ministry and Business

Nowadays, we say that people such as the eunuch, Aquila and Priscilla, who do church work while supporting themselves through secular jobs, are in part-time ministry. On the other hand, we consider pastors, evangelists and missionaries who do not have secular employment to be in full-time ministry. As a result of this arbitrary classification, leaving the marketplace has become a rite of passage for the transition into full-time ministry. This was not the norm in the Early Church. First-century Christians did not see working in the marketplace and serving in the Church as mutually exclusive activities. Paul, a full-time apostle, wrote to the Thessalonians that neither he nor his team members ate "anyone's bread without paying for it, but with labor and hardship [they] kept working night and day so that [they] might not be a burden to [anyone]" (2 Thess. 3:8). This is a clear reference to the fact that Paul and his ministry team did *secular* work while they ministered the Word. This was not an isolated incident, since Paul did the same thing while in Corinth as well as in Ephesus (see Acts 18:1-3).

Today we favor the notion that once the apostles left their secular jobs they never returned to them. However, Peter went back to fishing at least twice after he had been called by Jesus: the first time to get money for taxes (see Matt. 17:24-27) and the second time right after the Resurrection (see John 21:3). If a return to the marketplace was tantamount to backsliding and betraying his call to the ministry, as it is often taught, why would Jesus encourage such behavior by enabling Peter and his partners to catch so many fish? Luke was another prominent marketplace person. He is described by Paul as "the beloved physician" (Col. 4:14), an indication that he continued to practice medicine after he joined Paul's team.

Able to Produce Excellent Leaders
Community and marketplace people led the newly established churches and they were extraordinarily effective as elders, considering that most of them were appointed after a brief time of training and usually in a context of severe persecution. It is a wonder that Paul managed to be so effective in his selection of elders for the emerging congregations. The answer lies in the fact that after these folks, who were *already* leaders in the city, came to Christ—usually through a "power encounter"—they took positions of leadership in the Church. By "power encounter" I mean that they experienced the power of God when they were set free

from spiritual bondage, usually in a dramatic way, as in the case of the Philippi jailer (see Acts 16:25-34). This, in turn, resulted in Church leaders who knew God experientially rather than just intellectually and who were passionate about their newfound faith (see 1 Cor. 2:1-5). Consequently, they did more than simply sit on the board—they ministered to the flock and to the lost *on a daily basis* (see Acts 20:31).

Possible to Understand Theological Truths

The most controversial theological truth of the first century—that Gentiles can be saved without having to become Jews first—was initially presented to three marketplace leaders. Peter (food industry) was a guest at the home of Simon the tanner (leather goods) where Cornelius (a senior military officer) sent for him. This was a new and radical teaching for which the emerging Church had no paradigm. Nevertheless, God did not hesitate to entrust it to laymen. The fact that they had not been trained in theology at formal rabbinical schools, as the Pharisees had been trained, was an advantage given the unprecedented nature of the new revelation.

THE GROWTH OF THE CHURCH

When the time came to establish a missionary center from which the gospel would be spread to the ends of the earth, God moved the spiritual vortex of the Church from Jerusalem to Antioch, a merchant city located on the convergence of important trading roads.

Choosing Apostolic Coworkers

A common misconception among Christians is to view the seven men chosen in Acts chapter 6 as the equivalent of modern-day deacons. In many Bible translations the subtitle for this chapter is "Election of Deacons." However, the word "deacon" is not used in this passage as a noun to describe their role. Instead it is used as a verb to depict their function. The seven were never called deacons in the modern sense of the word. The task entrusted to them was far more elaborate than what we typically expect of deacons today. They were tapped to fix a deficiency in the system that fed thousands of people each day.

The Early Church was having a food-distribution problem that resulted in the neglect of some widows. Because these widows were part of an ethnic group that had previously been despised, tensions rose to the point of menacing the unity of the brethren. Worse yet, this happened "while the disciples were increasing in number" (Acts 6:1), undoubtedly threatening such growth. This was a problem that required immediate attention.

Solving Church Problems

The 12 apostles indicated that it was not desirable for them "to neglect the word of God in order to serve tables" (Acts 6:2). Because of this reference to *serving tables* many people assume that the seven men of good reputation noted in Acts 6:3 were chosen to do that. However, the criterion used to select what are sometimes called the Seven points to something more elaborate, since it called for men of good reputation (character) and full of the Spirit (spirituality) and of wisdom (capacity for the job at hand) to *be put in charge* of this task (managers).

Most likely the Seven were selected to fix the existing food-distribution problem because of their proven ability in business. There is no record that any of them served tables. In fact, two of them exited the picture shortly afterward: Stephen went to heaven and Philip left on an extensive evangelistic tour that transformed several cities (see Acts 7:60; 8:5-40).

The main point is that a problem important enough to be highlighted in the Scriptures was solved with great efficiency because recognized leaders in the congregation were selected to partner with the apostles. Furthermore, after the Seven were appointed, "the number of the disciples continued to increase greatly in Jerusalem" (Acts 6:7). It appears that their managerial expertise—once recognized and anointed by the apostles—solved a problem that was fast becoming a threat to the growth of the Church (see Acts 6:6-7).

Accelerating Evangelism Through Persecution

By this time the disciples had been in Jerusalem for more than 10 years and there had been no significant progress toward reaching the ends of the earth, except for forays into familiar territories such as Judea and Samaria. For the most part, the routine of these early Christians consisted of meeting house to house and in the Temple. Most likely the Temple (a building that defined Jerusalem) is what prevented them from moving outward, as Jesus had specified.

God eventually had to use persecution to force the Church to move out of Jerusalem. This in turn refocused their attention on the marketplace because they fled along trading routes that eventually led them to merchant centers such as Phoenicia, Cyprus and Antioch (see Acts 11:19-20). These were not isolated cases because the cities noted in Revelation were also commercial centers (see Rev. 2-3). It was not until the disciples were forced to leave Jerusalem that the Church began to make significant progress in its journey toward the ends of the earth.

Shaking Cities Through Paul's Marketplace Focus

From Paul's early missionary trips we learn that upon arriving in a city he first went to the local synagogue, if there was one (see Acts 13:5). However, the record of synagogues becoming churches is meager. In many cases Paul and his band of new believers were forced to exit the synagogue, and in many cases the city, under duress. This happened so many times that eventually Paul was led to focus on the Gentiles instead (see Acts 18:6). This happened in Corinth right after Paul had entered into a business partnership with Aquila and Priscilla (see Acts 18:1-3). He immediately moved his base of operation to a private house where he was able to teach daily, rather than just on the Sabbath, and many people believed and were baptized. In the midst of this spiritual harvest God spoke to Paul in a vision, alerting him that there were many believers *in the city*. It is interesting to note that God used this vision to point Paul to the city right after he had exited the synagogue. As a result, Paul settled in Corinth for a year and a half (see Acts 18:11).

This sequence of events is worth noticing since it shows Paul having shifted from the synagogue to the marketplace. First Paul entered the marketplace. Next he moved out of the synagogue to a nearby house. Then God alerted him to the fact that there were many believ-

ers *in the city*, rather than in the synagogue. This sequence was repeated in Ephesus, where he moved next, taking Aquila and Priscilla with
him (see Acts 18:18). The transition to the marketplace was accompanied in both cases by extraordinary results, specifically many conversions in the midst of dramatic power encounters.

Much of the economy of Ephesus was based upon demonic activities centered on the worship of goddesses, specifically Artemis, the fertility goddess who is also referred to as Diana.[2] This allowed Satan's
bunker to be firmly entrenched in the marketplace.

In this environment, Paul and his partners, Aquila and Priscilla,
entered the marketplace. They did it by setting up a tent-making operation (see Acts 20:33-35) and by using a secular venue, a school owned
by Tyrannus (see Acts 19:9-10), where they taught daily about the
kingdom of God. Two years later a dramatic power encounter caused
everyone in Ephesus *and the surrounding area* to hear the word of God
(see Acts 19:10). The spiritual atmosphere was so positive that God
was performing extraordinary miracles through Paul. This level of
supernatural occurrences had not been com-
mon until then, hence the extraordinary qual-
ifier. Even the demons acknowledged that
they knew who Paul was (see Acts 19:15).
Multitudes of people renounced their secret
practices, and leading practitioners of sorcery
burned their magic books. As a result, the
Word of the Lord grew and prevailed in a city
that had once been a major stronghold of
Satan (see Acts 19:20).

> There is no doubt
> that Ephesus
> was transformed
> by a power
> encounter that
> occurred *in the*
> *marketplace.*

There is no doubt that Ephesus was transformed by a power
encounter that occurred *in the marketplace*. Had Paul's ministry
remained confined to the synagogue, he never would have had such an
impact on a region as vast as the one he eventually did by establishing
roots in the marketplace. What happened in Ephesus was not exceptional; rather, it was normative. In fact, similar encounters must have
happened in other cities as well because later on Paul and his band were
accused of having done the same thing "all over Asia" (Acts 19:26).

THE CHURCH AS THE COUNTERCULTURE

Jesus' recruitment of marketplace people who were not members of the religious establishment was intentional. The same can be said about how the Holy Spirit led the Early Church to operate in the marketplace. The Great Commission begins with a city, Jerusalem, and it will be fulfilled when the last city on Earth is reached. To accomplish this, the city's most vital component, the marketplace, has to be transformed just as it happened in Ephesus and the other cities mentioned in Acts.

Because the marketplace embodies the societal systems that define and give life to a metropolis, Jesus recruited people from the marketplace to be the backbone of His redemptive movement. His objective was to create a new social vehicle—the Church, a movement that freely expanded, rather than a monument to be gazed at. This movement was meant to be the counterculture, rather than a subculture. People in a subculture are satisfied with surviving under the dominant culture, whereas those in a counterculture have as their *irretrievable* objective to debunk and replace it. According to the dictionary a counterculture is "a culture with values and mores that run counter to those of established society."[3]

This is why New Testament teaching is intentionally focused on curing social ills and repairing broken relationships as a means to transform society's institutions: marriage, family, work and government. This is true because Jesus' mission was not only to save individuals but also to bring people groups and nations to Himself (see Rev. 21:24-27). If He had come only to save people, believers would be transferred to heaven right after their conversions. Instead, they are left in the world and entrusted with the commission to disciple the nations.

TAKING THE KINGDOM OF GOD TO THE PEOPLE

Jesus always spoke of His disciples taking the kingdom of God to the people. He also compared His kingdom to leaven, light, salt and seeds. Each of these elements must come in contact with the physical world to fulfill its destiny: to infiltrate, shine, preserve or sprout. Jesus' design was for the Church to be the counterculture, not another subculture merely satisfied with survival.

This is where the marketplace comes into a sharper focus. Since business is what makes the marketplace go, we need to understand that the God of ministry is also the God of business. This is the subject of the next chapter.

Notes

1. The title "Most Excellent Theophilus" would seem to support the position that Theophilus was a high-ranking government leader. The *New English Bible* translates this expression "Your Excellency, Theophilus."
2. For more information on how the worship of Artemis and other goddesses affected Ephesus, read Clinton Arnold, *Power and Magic* (Grand Rapids, MI: Baker Book House, 1992).
3. *Merriam-Webster's Collegiate Dictionary*, 10th ed., s. v. "counterculture."

THE GOD OF BUSINESS

The expectations imposed upon Christian businesspeople resemble how women were treated during the Victorian era in regard to sex. They were told, "Do it, but do not enjoy it. Produce results [children], but do not get too excited in the process lest you become sensuous." Likewise, believers in the marketplace are expected to make a profit, but they are not supposed to feel too good about it for fear of becoming materialistic.

The majority of the Old Testament heroes were not ascetics; rather, they were people deeply involved in everyday marketplace issues. Abraham, "the father of the faith" (Rom. 4:1), carried that spiritual mantle without giving up his very prosperous earthly occupation. In fact, he was one of the most successful and wealthy businessmen in the ancient Near East (see Gen. 12–25). Job—the head of a family business— was the wealthiest man in the country of Uz (see Job 1:3), where he was very active in societal and governmental issues (see Job 31).

Most prophets in the Old Testament, with the notable exceptions of Eli and Samuel, were businessmen who did not support themselves with traditional Levitical resources. They saw the hand of God in their business deals as much as they did around the altar. David is a classic example. He told Saul that God provided security services for his shepherding business by empowering him to kill the lions and bears that came to decimate his inventory. To David, God's protection was an integral part of his business (see 1 Sam. 17:34-37).

To better understand this factor I will take a novel look at the story of David and Goliath. I want to examine the *business dimension* of this epic encounter, which we traditionally spiritualize to the point of obscuring its significance as it relates to the marketplace.

THE TINY CATERER AND THE GIANT

One of the greatest victories recorded in the Bible pitted a small businessman against a professional soldier. Through sheer intimidation, Goliath had immobilized the people of God for 40 days before David, a junior partner in a family-owned husbandry business, showed up (see 1 Sam. 17:15-19). David, who had taken on the cloak of a caterer, went to the battlefield to deliver food to his brothers. He arrived in time to hear Goliath's challenge and to witness Saul's soldiers panic.

David, a godly man, was incensed by Goliath's taunt to the armies of the living God and by the reproach it represented. But because he was also a businessman, what caught his attention next was that a reward (profit) had been offered. He asked, "What will be done for the man who kills this Philistine?" (1 Sam. 17:26). What David appears to have been thinking was, *This giant is an uncircumcised Philistine, and we are the armies of the living God. There is no way that Goliath can ever win because God is on our side. Victory is a sure thing. Why let a good reward go to waste?*

God in the Marketplace

David did not see a conflict, or an incompatibility, between a spiritual assignment and a financial reward. Unfortunately, today when we retell his story we emphasize his zeal for the Lord but inadvertently suppress any mention of his interest in the recompense, as if the latter were an evil deed. This represents a great injustice, because dichotomizing the spiritual and the material did not enter the mind of David—someone who was described by Samuel as "a man after God's heart" (1 Sam. 13:14). For David, the parallel he drew between God's protection in his business and in the impending encounter with Goliath was absolutely natural. He expected God to be with him in this undertaking just as He was with him when he fought off the lions. He did not believe that fighting Goliath was a spiritual enterprise and running his business a secular one. God was central in both of them.

An Old Myth About Businesspeople

David's oldest brother, Eliab, tried to disqualify him from any role on the battlefield on account of his occupation: "With whom have you left those few sheep in the wilderness?" (1 Sam. 17:28). He accused David of having impure motives and told him to go back to his business. Eliab did not believe that David belonged with the pros. In other words, what he meant was, *You have no right to comment on our lack of results because your training is in business. Go back and take care of it so that you can keep on funding us, but don't tell us what to do!*

Does this sound familiar? If you work in the marketplace, you have probably heard something like this somewhere along the way in your Christian life: "Let the professionals do the ministry and you take care of business."

A Familiar Ring

David turned away from Eliab and kept asking others the *same* question. Obviously his inquiry had to do with the reward because "the people answered the *same* thing as before" (1 Sam. 17:30, emphasis added). David must have displayed confidence that Goliath could and should be defeated and made known his interest in the reward because "when the words which David spoke were heard, they told them to Saul, and he sent for him" (1 Sam. 17:31). David knew that the deal was morally right, a sure thing *and* profitable. Consequently, he was convinced that it should be pursued.

Profit Motive Not Necessarily Evil

David's interest in the reward must not be overlooked because it touches on a very sensitive issue: the profit motive. The profit motive is to a businessperson what the drive to win is to an athlete.[1] No athlete worth his or her salt enters a competition to lose. To the contrary, they always expect to win. It is such determination that allows him or her to overcome extraordinary obstacles. In the same manner, the profit motive provides the stimulus needed for a businessperson to tackle similar challenges in the marketplace. It is a gift from God that, when used within proper boundaries, can benefit millions of people.

> The profit motive is to a businessperson what the drive to win is to an athlete.

However, when an athlete tries to win at any cost, he or she becomes destructive. The same is true of a businessperson whose motivation is to profit no matter how he or she does it. The drive to win and the desire to make a profit are given by God to provide the incentive required for conquering exceptional challenges. But both must be exercised according to God's overarching principles. To win or to profit in an unethical manner or outside the will of God is never right. In fact, its consequences are devastating. The pitfalls of unbridled capitalism are many, including slavery, child labor and underpaid workers. It is not just how profit is made that is important but also the purpose for making a profit (which I will cover later in this book).

While we need to be mindful of these cautions, they should not cause us to perceive profit as intrinsically evil. In fact, it is this misconception that prevents many Christians from making it big in business. Deep down they are not sure that they can be successful and godly at the same time. This ambivalence causes them to get lost in a maze of self-doubts. They struggle with who they are in the marketplace—businesspeople—and have trouble recognizing the validity of the tool provided God for them to succeed—profit motive. As a result, many marketplace Christians remain in business but give up on experiencing the joy of the Lord in their work or of significant success, as if the former was impossible and the latter undesirable or, worse yet, evil.

This is a terrible way to live. The expectations imposed upon Christian businesspeople resemble how women were treated during the Victorian era in regard to sex. Godly women were supposed to do it but not to enjoy it. It was their responsibility to produce results (children) but not to get too excited in the process lest they become sensuous. Likewise, believers in the marketplace are expected to make a profit, but they are not supposed to feel too good about it for fear of becoming materialistic.

There is nothing intrinsically wrong with sex or with profit. God designed both of them for an honorable purpose. The fact that either can be abused should not prevent us from appreciating and exercising the divine intent behind them. God attaches pleasure to vital functions such as procreating and eating to ensure that they are exercised. In the business world, profit motive serves that purpose by functioning as the incentive that keeps business happening.

In the case of Christian businesspeople, the devil seeks to thwart this motivation. By labeling believers as "profit-driven" in a demeaning way, he either keeps them away from the marketplace or handicaps them with self-doubt if they choose to enter it. This is why it is refreshing, and even healing, to study David's approach.

Business Experience Applied to Spiritual Challenges
When Saul disqualified David because of his lack of professional training, David brought up a principle he had used successfully in business. He told the king how he went after the lions and bears that attacked his livestock, recovered what was stolen and killed the predators. We tend to spiritualize what he said, but David is describing how he dealt with the equivalent of modern-day shoplifting, except that instead of junior

high students doing it, it was wild animals that carried it out. Facing bears and lions with bare hands and recovering stolen goods was no small feat, but David candidly told Saul that he was able to do it because God was involved. From his past success, he wisely concluded that God would also be with him when he faced Goliath.

David did not use Saul's armor, opting for the tools of his trade instead—a staff, a sling and stones. Goliath despised and cursed David because of this. David did not let those insults intimidate him. He was comfortable with his equipment because he had seen God empower him every time he used it to protect his business. The situation at hand was no different. He reasoned that the same anointing that operated in shepherding should also work against the champion of the devil. And it did!

GOD'S LOVE AND CARE FOR THE WORLD

It is necessary to rediscover the principle behind David's approach. He saw God deeply interested in everything he did, whether he was watching his flock, catering food for the soldiers or fighting the evil giant. His job was his ministry and his ministry was his job—both happened in a context of intense spiritual warfare. Please, notice that both David and Goliath saw their encounter as a spiritual struggle. Goliath cursed David by his gods, and David replied with a challenge exalting Jehovah (see 1 Sam. 17:43-47). Even though they were dealing with swords, javelin, armor, slings and stones, they both knew that this was a spiritual confrontation.

Nowadays we have dichotomized the material and spiritual worlds. We have wrongly concluded that the intangible realm is more likely to be filled with good things, while the tangible world—the one where we spend the *totality* of our earthly life—is intrinsically evil. This distinction is not found in the Scriptures. We have come to rate plowing a field or entering a business transaction in the general ledger as less valid than meditation, prayer or praise. But the former are expressions of life on Earth that when done unto the glory of God are as spiritually valid as the latter. God created the world and every material thing in it; and when

He was done with His creation, He pronounced it "very good" (Gen. 1:31). God loves the world so much that He gave the very best—His only begotten Son—to provide the means of salvation from the evil defilement of all things, human and material, that was introduced by Satan. God is compassionate about both His creatures and His creation. Nineveh is a good example of this. God sent Jonah to call this city to repentance because He cared not just about the people who lived there but also about the animals (see Jonah 4:11).

The world has been contaminated by sin and continues to deteriorate because of a preponderance of it. But God has provided a way to reverse this course:

> [If] my people humble themselves and pray, and seek My face and turn from their wicked ways, then I will hear from heaven, will forgive their sin, and will heal their land! (2 Chron. 7:14).

The land this verse refers to is the land we live on. But it does not just mean the land; it also means the economy it sustains and everything else that emanates from it, all of which have been defiled by sin. No one appreciates the need for the healing of the land more than people in the marketplace, because they are the ones who constantly struggle with what sin has brought about.

No one appreciates the need for the healing of the land more than people in the marketplace.

Why the Devil Fears Marketplace People

All through the Bible we see how people in the marketplace, who operated under the power of God, inflicted serious damage to the devil's empire. Joseph, Moses, Job, Gideon, David, Daniel, Esther, Elijah, Peter, Paul, Barnabas and many others upset his evil plans. This is why today the devil is afraid that Christians will fulfill their divine destiny in the marketplace and bring the kingdom of God to it. To prevent this from happening he constantly disqualifies them by debasing their occupation—telling them that it is less spiritual than Church work—and He paints them as materialistic and unspiritual. The devil fears the knowledge of what makes a city tick and operational efficiency that marketplace Christians are capable of bringing to Kingdom expansion.

This efficiency is vividly illustrated by the no-nonsense approach used by the Roman centurion when he asked Jesus to heal his servant. Because the centurion understood operational systems, he knew how to delegate power: "Just say the word, and my servant will be healed. For I, too, am a man under authority, with soldiers under me; and I say to this one, 'Go!' and he goes, and to another, 'Come!' and he comes" (Matt. 8:8-9). He was very appreciative of Jesus' time and did not want to waste any of it. Jesus was so impressed by the centurion's approach that He bestowed on him an *extraordinary* compliment, "I have not found such great faith with anyone in Israel" (Matt. 8:10). This Gentile marketplace leader had a level of faith not seen anywhere else. This incident illustrates why business, education and government leaders need to be incorporated into the leadership of the church.

Efficiency as a Norm

I have often seen situations where problems that have frustrated pastors for years are solved in a few days when businesspeople are brought on board as ministry *peers*. This happens because efficiency is an absolute must in the marketplace. The competitive nature of the environment in which businesspeople operate daily does not tolerate error or even vacillation, because if too many deals go wrong they get fired. These people do not have the option of telling the board or the shareholders, "It was the will of God that we lose money," or "The devil interfered with our plans." They are required to consistently operate at the highest level of efficiency possible.

When their natural ability to identify the bottom line and to troubleshoot are framed by personal *good reputation, faith* and *wisdom,* as was the case of the Seven in Acts, the word of the Lord spreads and the number of disciples increases (see Acts 6:7). The growth is so great that even people in groups that had previously been unresponsive suddenly get saved. For example, in Acts 6:7 it is recorded that "a great many of the priests were becoming obedient to the faith." This is due in part to the influence marketplace leaders had in the city.

Your Divine Destiny

Marketplace Christians, take heart! You have the same spiritual capacity that the Roman centurion had—actually even a greater one because you live on this side of Calvary and the Resurrection. With so much divine power at your disposal you are expected, in fact commanded, to do greater works than even Jesus did (see John 14:12-15). Do not confine yourself to a spectator's seat from which you only watch ministry happen. If you do, Satan will continue to run rampant in your city. However, the day you discover that you have a divine call along with the anointing and the jurisdiction to exercise it in the marketplace, God's kingdom will begin to replace Satan's in the heart of your city.

For the Glory of God

It is important not to let the evil one disqualify you on account of your occupation. He will repeatedly tell you that because your focus is on the marketplace, you have no right to be in ministry. He will try to convince you that you should be in business solely to make a living and that the marketplace has no transcendent purpose. But being in business for the glory of God adds the most sublime purpose to your occupation. *Do not let your occupation block your destiny; instead, allow your destiny to shape your business by turning it into your ministry.*

If you are going to accomplish this, a compelling understanding and embracing of God's purpose is crucial, especially if you find yourself in difficult straits. Do not let negative circumstances immobilize you. Do not be an echo of disappointing factors when, with God's help, you can be a prophetic voice that calls into being what is still unseen. God's purpose for you is immutable, and you have the full power of heaven at your disposal to fulfill it (see John 14:14; Phil. 4:13). Fix your eyes upon the goal and, in faith, take that first step today. The key is to get moving regardless of where you find yourself at this moment. That first step is the most difficult but also the most crucial because it will propel you in the direction of your destiny. Remember, He who began the good work in you will complete it. He always does.

Your current occupation or your station in your field does not matter. Jesus began as a carpenter, David as the shepherd of a small flock and Peter as a fisherman. Those were small beginnings, yet each of them fulfilled their divine destiny and affected millions of lives. Jesus hung on a tree and carved the lives of millions into replicas of Himself. David became the shepherd of Israel. Peter turned into the premier fisher of men. If you are a Christian in the marketplace, unsure of your role, listen to the Holy Spirit *now*. He is the One who is assigned to lead you to all truth. Let Him touch the innermost part of your soul and bring to light those areas darkened by man-made shame and confusion. Never let negative circumstances determine your destiny. Instead, change those circumstances by wholeheartedly embracing your divine purpose.

Let God show you that your parish, your congregation, your flock is in fact the marketplace. There is a purpose and a destiny for you there. You are part of a movement God has designed to bring His kingdom to the heart of the city. You can take your first step toward your destiny right now, because the God of ministry is also the God of business!

Note

1. Profit motive also applies to the other components of the marketplace (government and education), although not as centrally as it does to business. The main thrusts in education are ideas and knowledge. In government, it is the provision of vital services. However, schools need to have enough income to stay open and governments need to generate enough revenue to fund their programs.

CHAPTER 5

GOD LOVES BILL GATES, TOO

If a homeless lady dressed in dirty old rags and covered with ulcers walks into a revival meeting, she will instantly become the object of compassion. No one will doubt that God wants to transform her life—right away. On the other hand, if a rich man dressed in an Armani suit and tanned from a vacation in the Bahamas enters the same revival, very few people will believe that God has the same level of interest in meeting his needs.

I had looked forward to the youth retreat like a prisoner anticipates his release. It was going to be the first time since my conversion that I would be able to spend a week in the presence of God with no interruptions and receive ministry from experienced teachers. My expectations could not have been higher.

During the opening session I listened to the testimony of a woman who had been very successful in her secular career. She told us how, after she became a believer, she had burned her college diplomas and thrown away all her books. Amidst approving nods and an enthusiastic chorus of amens, she stressed how important it is for Christians not to dwell in Egypt when we have the option to walk in the wilderness with God. She told story after story about believers who had ended up stuck forever in the filthy mire of the world after they had been lured into pursuing secular careers rather than full-time ministry. Many of those people became extremely rich but left their walk with God. Her unmistakably clear message was "Be poor and godly rather than rich and worldly."

I was so touched by her challenge that upon returning home I told my father that I wanted to quit my studies and immediately go into full-time ministry. I explained to him that Jesus was coming back soon, that this world was going to burn and that every day counted.

My father was not yet a believer, but he was very wise and successful. He put his hand on my shoulder and told me, "Son, I do not know much about the Bible or about Jesus Christ, and much less about this return of His that you are so sure about. But this I know: Studying and working hard has never hurt anyone. You have a good head and an excellent record, so far. So stay with it and don't ever raise this stupid idea again, because if you do, *I will break your neck!*"

I was blown away by his bluntness and, in self-defense, I began to babble passionately about the risks that success in the world entails and how I did not believe God could trust me to remain humble once I succeeded. He locked his gaze on me and declared: "Son, the only people that have a shot at humility are those who succeed. The ones who fail have already been humbled by their failure. Go on, succeed, and then humble yourself by turning it over to the Lord. Listen to what I am saying and do it, or what I said a few moments ago about what may happen to your neck will be upgraded from a *probability* to a *certainty*."

Looking back, I now realize that his straightforward input was the best career counseling I ever got and, even though he did not know it and did not clothe it in Christian phraseology, it was biblical.

WEALTH, POWER AND FAME: GETTING IT STRAIGHT

Two common misconceptions often prevent godly Christians from moving enthusiastically into the marketplace with the clear intent and necessary determination to succeed. The Church widely, although perhaps unintentionally, teaches or, at least, implies that God despises rich people and that success is something Christians cannot handle well. These lies need to be debunked.

Significant perils result from the improper handling of wealth. Jesus did not approve of the rich man who dressed in purple and fine linen and refused to share with Lazarus, the beggar, even the crumbs that fell from his luxurious table (see Luke 16:19-31). Paul admonishes wealthy Christians not to put their hope in riches but to be generous and ready to share (see 1 Tim. 6:17-19). James rebuked greedy rich people who sat on their wealth until it rusted while their workers' wages went unpaid (see Jas. 5:1-6). But none of these cases represents a condemnation of rich people per se—only those who mishandled their wealth.

How does God really feel about the rich?

The Bible unequivocally declares that God loves the world and gave His Son so that whosoever believes in Him would not perish but have everlasting life (see John 3:16). The whole world was *and remains* the object of His love, and the gateway to salvation is open to whosoever. The two words "world" and "whosoever" are inclusive terms. God loves everybody and does not make a distinction based on race, gender or social status.

Unfortunately, when it comes to the social divide between the rich and the poor, the Church often exhibits a negative bias toward the rich, the result of ascribing innate virtue to poverty while suspecting intrinsic vices in wealth. This is clearly seen in missionary priorities. The church that enthusiastically sends missionaries to a tiny hidden group in the

Amazon will rarely consider sending one to the thousands of sinners living in Monaco or the millions in Sweden, mostly because of the wealth in those countries. This has resulted in a faulty set of priorities, because people in wealthy nations are just as lost as natives in the Third World. The thought of resident missionaries in Beverly Hills or Monte Carlo is considered borderline blasphemy. This view, however, does not match up with what Jesus did. He was a friend of all sinners, wealthy and destitute alike. He loved and ministered to both. The way in which He conducted Himself in Jericho illustrates this point.

Jericho: A Case Study in Social Reconciliation

Before entering Jericho Jesus healed Bartimaeus, a beggar who most likely was the poorest and neediest person in the city. As soon as Jesus made it through the gates, He ministered to Zacchaeus, one of the wealthiest men in town.

However, when word got out about Jesus' intention to be a guest in Zacchaeus's home, disappointment, even anger, engulfed the crowd that had just praised God when Bartimaeus was healed (see Luke 18:43). This prompted Jesus to explain Zacchaeus's eligibility for salvation: "He, too, is a son of Abraham. For the Son of Man has come to seek and to save that which was lost" (Luke 19:9-10). The adverb "too" refers back to Bartimaeus. Jesus stated that both men, regardless of their social positions, unequivocally stood on level ground before God and, consequently, salvation was offered *equally* to both of them.

The inhabitants of Jericho had no problem believing that a poor blind beggar deserved a miracle, but they were not sure about a wealthy tax collector whom they openly despised as a sinner. The inference is that Bartimaeus was not considered to be a sinner or, at least, not as much of a sinner as Zacchaeus. However, there is no scriptural evidence to indicate that Bartimaeus was either a godly person or a sinner. We do not know if he helped other beggars or if he stole money from them. Since the Scriptures do not describe him as godly, it is entirely possible that he was as much of a sinner as Zacchaeus. On the other hand, even though Zacchaeus's contemporaries openly called him a sinner, *Jesus never did.* The Lord knew that both men needed salvation (see Luke 19:9).

Bill Gates: A Contemporary Zacchaeus?

The lesson Jesus taught in Jericho needs to be learned anew because in the Church today there is a strong prejudice against the rich and a clear tilt toward the poor when it comes to the idea of God's willingness to meet people's *felt* needs. For instance, if a homeless lady dressed in dirty old rags and covered with ulcers walks into a revival meeting, she will become the object of *instant* compassion. No one will doubt that God wants to do something to transform her life—right away. On the other hand, if Bill Gates were to walk into the same setting, very few people, if any at all, will believe that God had the *same* level of interest in helping him. They will probably suspect Gates's motives for coming to church or gawk at him as a celebrity. Nevertheless, Bill Gates has needs that for him are as important and urgent as the ones the homeless lady has in her life. For example, Gates's company is constantly buffeted by lawsuits, and he has the responsibility of being a husband and raising two young children. Could he use prayer for both his business and home life? Does God want to transform both? More important, both the homeless lady and a man as rich as Bill Gates clearly have the eternal need of salvation.

We often fail to see the innermost needs of the rich and famous because of a bias that ascribes virtue to poverty and innate evil to wealth. This way of thinking leads to the assumptions that poor people have greater needs than wealthy people do and that the rich can take care of themselves. Jesus did not think this way. That is why He sought out Zacchaeus as well as Bartimaeus. And that is why today He seeks out people such as Bill Gates, as well as the homeless lady.

God's Plan for the Rich

It is obvious that the Lord's statement did not convince the crowd in Jericho, because He had to explain Himself further with a parable. The way the parable was introduced—"And while they were listening to these things, He went on to tell a parable"—shows that it was meant to address the crowd's prejudice against Zacchaeus. The words "these things" connect Jesus' affirming words about the tax collector with the parable He was about to present. He told the parable of the ten minas for two reasons: to validate Zacchaeus's eligibility for salvation and to explain the key role that wealthy people such as him would play in establishing God's kingdom in cities all over the world.

The second reason is revealed in the next sentence: "Because He was near Jerusalem they supposed that the kingdom of God was going to appear immediately" (Luke 19:11). Jesus saw the need to clarify that God's kingdom would not appear *immediately* in one place; rather, *progressively* in many cities.

> **We often fail to see the innermost needs of the rich and famous because of a bias that ascribes virtue to poverty and innate evil to wealth.**

This parable is about a nobleman who goes away from his home in order to have his right to the kingdom certified. This is a reference to Jesus during the Church Age, a season when He is waiting for all things to be put under His feet (see Acts 2:34-35). Before going away, the nobleman entrusted his servants with a certain amount of money with which to do business. While he was gone, the citizens rebelled against him, but this did not prevent his servants from conducting business or making a profit.

Upon the nobleman's return, "he ordered that these slaves, to whom he had given the money, be called to him in order that he might know what business they had done" (Luke 19:15). To the one who reported a yield of 10 minas he gave authority over 10 cities. To the one who gained five, he granted the same over five cities. After rebuking the one who refused to invest his capital, the nobleman had his own enemies brought in and they were slain in his presence (see Luke 19:20-27). It was at that moment that the nobleman took control of the kingdom to which he had held title all along.

Three Dangerous Misconceptions

In the parable of the ten minas, there are three key points that need to be highlighted:

1. The nobleman's servants prospered in business, even though his enemies had usurped the kingdom.

2. The nobleman gave his servants authority over cities in direct proportion to the return on their investment.
3. The nobleman did not destroy his enemies until he had placed his servants over cities.

To fully understand the lessons emanating from these points, it is necessary to keep in mind that Jesus told this parable to correct the following three misperceptions:

1. Rich businesspeople such as Zacchaeus have no place in the kingdom of God, or at least not important places.
2. The kingdom of God would materialize suddenly, rather than as a result of a process.
3. The kingdom of God would appear in one place, Jerusalem, rather than in cities all over the world.

Excesses That Lead to Heresy

Eschatology is the theological study of the future, of events yet to come. Lack of balance in our eschatological view regarding the Lord's return is the cause for these three misconceptions. Since we already know the final outcome—Jesus' triumphant return to Earth to dwell with His people in the New Jerusalem—we interpret all other relevant Scriptures through this majestic final event and fail to pay attention to and become fully engaged in the process leading up to it.

It is like reading the last chapter of a mystery novel first. Everything we read afterwards will be seen through the ending we already know. This will cause us not to spend adequate time processing less clear sections, since we already know the final outcome. Likewise, as Christians we believe that Jesus is coming back to rule the world and that He will dwell in the New Jerusalem with us. There is such a strong focus on this wonderful outcome that we brush aside anything having to do with the less wonderful world in which we find ourselves today. In such a context it is very easy to write off other cities and places where the kingdom of God needs to be established as an important stepping-stone toward that majestic climax. As evangelical Christians, we are notorious for our lack of concern and care for the world in which we live. Because we expect new heavens and a new Earth, it is as if we have abdicated our social and cultural responsibility.

By doing this we are no different than the people to whom Jesus addressed the parable of the ten minas: We expect the kingdom of God to materialize suddenly and in one place. Even though this is true—it will happen in Jerusalem when Jesus returns in glory—in the meantime, there is much that has to take place in cities all over the world in preparation for that climax.

Finding a Solution

What is it that needs to be done?

Servants loyal to the returning King (Jesus) need to enter the marketplace and use whatever He has entrusted to them to gain authority through their success. They must do this even though His enemies control the marketplace. Their presence and eventual success will produce a progressive manifestation of the kingdom of God as they bring a *measure* of it to the heart of the city. The *fullness* will come later when the Lord returns to dwell with His people in the New Jerusalem which is the ultimate centerpiece: "The nations shall walk by its light, and the kings of the earth shall bring their glory into it" (Rev. 21:24). We know that these are godly kings and nations because a few verses further John elaborates: "Nothing unclean, and no one who practices abomination and lying, shall ever come into (Jerusalem), *but only those whose names are written in the Lamb's book of life*" (Rev. 21:27, emphasis added).

The king's servants prospered because the assignment given to them was intrinsically good and as such *capable of overcoming evil*. Notice how disappointed the king was with the slave who failed to invest, even at the passive level of a savings account. The key to the king's approval was each servant's willingness to use the capital entrusted to him in spite of having to operate in enemy-held territory. The reward was authority over cities. It is important not to miss this: authority over cities was granted in direct proportion to business success that came about as a result of obedience.

In the parable of the ten minas, Jesus highlighted a very important point: Rich people need to be saved so that they can bring the kingdom of God to their cities by practicing God's economics like Zacchaeus did and *eventually* assume positions of authority so that the Kingdom will be made manifest. This kind of authority is not mandated; rather, it is earned. A person gains it through servanthood, just as Jesus did (see Phil. 2:5-11). By using their resources to take care of the needy (showing generosity) and to right wrongs (applying justice), they are bound to have an impact on cities. If Zacchaeus had lived today, he would be a regular guest on *Larry King Live* and would appear on the cover of *Time* magazine. The impact of his actions would eloquently show the kingdom of God for everyone to see.

The Awarding of Authority over Cities

There is a significant difference between being awarded a kingdom and taking control of it. Today the Lord is seated at the right hand of the Father, interceding for us while He waits for all things to be put under His feet. Jesus has the title but not yet the fullness of the earthly Kingdom awarded to Him (see Acts 2:34-35).

> Rich people need to be saved so that they can bring the kingdom of God to their cities.

According to this parable, to take control of this Kingdom requires true, tried and trusted servants to be placed in positions of authority over cities. This is where people such as Zacchaeus come into play. He was a businessman who, upon switching allegiances, immediately brought to the marketplace the ethics of his new King by making restitution to those he may have defrauded and by giving half of his possessions to the poor. No one else in Jericho could have had such a powerful impact on the city. Before Zacchaeus's encounter with Jesus, his wealth was the object of intense contempt, yet the moment he was freed from greed, his wealth became his most powerful weapon against the evil motivation that previously controlled him.

The New Zacchaeus

Unfortunately when it comes to Zacchaeus, we are so fixated with his past—a despised dwarfish tax collector—that we miss the extraordinary good he did only minutes after coming into the kingdom of God. We also fail to grasp the earth-shaking consequences of his actions.

Let's imagine for a moment what the world would be like if other rich people were to emulate Zacchaeus? For once, government institutions would not lack resources, since taxes would be paid promptly and honestly. Poverty would be eradicated if 50 percent of the capital currently held by only 2 percent of the population were to be invested to help the people struggling in the bottom 20 percent of the income bracket. Wealth is a gift from God, but it needs to be brought under the power and the authority of our Lord. Redeemed wealth has a key role in God's plans to establish His kingdom on Earth.

I am not advocating some form of Christian socialism; rather, I am encouraging Christians to acknowledge God as the source of wealth and to see wealth as a resource that God will renew every time it is used to bless needy people. Such an understanding would bring poor and rich people together. Let us not forget that when Zacchaeus announced that he would give half of what he owned to the poor, one of the primary beneficiaries was Bartimaeus.

Poverty Versus Wealth

It is not productive to pit wealth and poverty against each other. I am going to use an extreme example to illustrate this point. Some churches concentrate their ministry on the rich while others focus on the poor. People in each congregation have plenty of spite for each other. The outcome has been, on one hand, compassionate ministries that are perpetually broke and, on the other hand, well-funded ones that are nonetheless broke, having few opportunities or little desire to do good. The latter, in order to cope with the guilt that arises from self-centered actions, needs to constantly come up with clever hermeneutical acrobatics to show that Christians can be rich and unconcerned about systemic poverty and indulge themselves in the pleasures of the world all the way to the pearly gates. People who resent the rich engage in a similar exercise from the opposite direction: they teach that God despises wealth, yet simultaneously they constantly cry over their lack of resources on their journey to the same pearly gates.

A Level Playing Field

Jesus understands both the rich and the poor because He *fully* identified with each group. Paul, in a passage dealing with the material transfer of wealth, wrote that Jesus, being rich, for our sake became poor so that through His poverty we might become rich (see 2 Cor. 8:9). If Jesus was opposed to the rich, why would He want to make us rich? And if being poor were a dishonorable state, why would He adopt it?

The answer lies with the fact that Jesus was never owned by or exclusively associated with either group. Consequently, He was free to move from one end of the social spectrum to the other with so much ease that He gave the impression that there were no demarcation lines. Jesus' parents gave the poor man's offering when they presented Him in the Temple, yet He was laid to rest in the sepulchre of a rich man (see Isa. 53:9; Matt. 27:57-60). He was the guest of wealthy people, yet He rode into Jerusalem on somebody else's donkey to have the Last Supper in a borrowed venue. He gave Peter and his friends a bonus catch of fish but later on allowed them to eat the remnants of a harvested field—a Mosaic concession to the poor (see Lev. 19:9-10).

Flunking the Wealth Test

Jesus never opposed wealth, per se. What He objected to was idle wealth and the control it can exercise on those who have it. This is clearly seen in the dialogue He had with the rich ruler. This young man owned much property (see Mark 10:22) and was extremely rich (see Luke 18:23), yet Jesus "felt love for him" (Mark 10:21). The Lord told him, "Sell all that you possess, and distribute it to the poor; and you shall have a treasure in heaven; and come follow Me" (Luke 18:22). Sadly, this person who was good enough to meet Jesus' recruitment standards did not make the cut because he was not willing to invest his wealth in the poor.

Why did Jesus tell him to sell his possessions? He did not do it because wealth is evil but because the young man was controlled by it. Jesus did not suggest that the man give his wealth to the poor so that he would also become poor; rather, such an action would have been an affirmation of God as the *source* and the *replenisher* of wealth as a *means* to bless people. The key issues were ones of perspective and trust. Did the young ruler understand, or have the *perspective*, that his wealth was not his but that God had entrusted it to him for a purpose? No. Was he willing to *trust* God to replenish the wealth once he had given it away? No.

God's perspective becomes clear when we read that right after the young rich man departed, Jesus assured Peter that because he had chosen to follow the Lord, he would "receive many times as much at this time and in the age to come, eternal life" (Luke 18:28). Peter stood to be entrusted with *more*, not less, wealth; but it was not meant to be hoarded; it was given so Peter could do good with it. The rich man's problem was his inability to see wealth as a means to benefit the poor, instead of a crutch to shore up his own insecurities or to define his identity.

Wealth: Blessing or Curse?

Paul admonished "those who are rich . . . not to be conceited or to fix their hope on the uncertainty of riches but on God, who richly supplies us with all things to enjoy" (1 Tim. 6:17). Paul does not condemn wealth or the pleasure that wealth brings. In fact, He presents God as a generous provider and tells the rich to enjoy His provision. Wealth is not the problem, but attachment to it is: "For the *love* of money is a root of all sorts of evil" (1 Tim. 6:10, emphasis added).

This attachment is extremely deceitful because it makes people think that they own wealth, when in reality it is the wealth that owns them. This in turn causes them to devote the bulk of their time and energy to maintaining wealth, instead of *liberally* using it to do good. This is why Paul wrote, "Instruct [the rich] to do good, to be rich in good works, to be generous and ready to share, storing up for themselves the treasure of a good foundation for the future, so that they may take hold of that which is life indeed" (1 Tim. 5:18-19). Paul clearly implies that the very foundation for life is built by doing good and being generous with those in need.

God entrusts people with riches to bless others because wealth is a *renewable* resource and He is the generous replenisher. When believers are controlled by wealth, they fail to enter the kingdom of God and miss life itself. They will still go to heaven, but they will miss experiencing the kingdom of God on Earth. This is true even in churches where the leaders dream up and fund programs that have more to do with membership indulgence than with Kingdom focus.

Wealth has to be seen as a trust, and it has to be used liberally to bless others as a practical expression of our belief that God is the provider and the replenisher. Doing otherwise brings spiritual misery. Look how poorly the young ruler did compared to Zacchaeus. He failed to enter the kingdom of God whereas Zacchaeus had the kingdom of God. If enough born-again Zacchaeuses enter the picture, the oozing gap alienating those who have too much and those who have too little will be closed. Better yet, the societal iniquities that result from such a gap will be corrected. Since we live in an imperfect and sinful way, those iniquities will not be removed completely, but the benefits will constitute a tangible expression of God's will being done on Earth. This is why the first social action undertaken by the Early Church was to take care of the poor. Bridging this gap is essential for the realization of kingdom of God, as we will see in the next chapter.

CHAPTER 6

RECONCILIATION IN THE MARKETPLACE

*Reconciliation is a matter of binding those who are
different with the love of Jesus Christ.*

FORMER PRESIDENT JIMMY CARTER, HABITAT WORLD

The honor and the dishonor of a city are reflected in the marketplace. If there is justice, that is where it will show the most. If there is corruption, or social injustice, the marketplace will reveal it. A human face may be nice, proportionate and well-designed, but an ugly wound would defile it. Misery is such a wound. Worse yet, misery in a context of grave social injustices, oppression and selfishness on the part of the rich turns that ugly wound into an oozing one.

Marketplace Christianity can heal that wound and replace it with unblemished beauty. In the New Testament this was accomplished, not just by the redistribution of wealth—from the rich to the poor—but by actions that demonstrated that the rich were no longer controlled by their possessions and that the poor were welcome into their circles. This is clearly seen in the reports of life in the Early Church. Rich and poor people ate together with joy and simplicity of heart, making sure that no one lacked anything (see Acts 2:42-47; 4:32-35). Evidently a very important gap had been bridged—the marketplace gap.

SIX SOCIAL GAPS

In the epistle to the Ephesians, Paul identifies six social gaps that need to be bridged before the Church can confront the rulers of the darkness over this world (see Eph. 6:12). This is a direct reference to the power that the devil and his evil empire exercise over the lost. This confrontation is not an abstract one but one designed to wrestle control from them. However, for the Church to be successful, it must first take care of these gaps.

- Ethnic (see Eph. 2:13-22): Paul explains how Jews and Gentiles have been reconciled in Christ. They are now "built together into a dwelling of God in the Spirit" (v. 22), which leaves no room for any other ethnic division.
- Denominational (see Eph. 3:16-21): This section teaches that when saints are rooted and grounded in love, they are able to comprehend the love of God through a supernatural knowledge that causes them to be filled "up to the fullness of God" (v. 19).

This divine fullness preempts the legitimacy of any human-made division.

- Ministerial (see Eph. 4:1-6): Apostles, prophets, evangelists, pastors and teachers are exhorted to "preserve the unity of the Spirit in the bond of peace" (v. 3). This unity does not have to be created. It already exists, thus the exhortation to maintain it.
- Gender (see Eph. 5:21-33): This is the oldest human division, the one that divides men and women, particularly husbands and wives (v. 33). This passage teaches how to bridge it through mutual submission (see v. 21) that results in unconditional love on the part of husbands and unlimited respect on the part of wives (v. 33). In my book *Women: God's Secret Weapon* I explain in depth how this works out in everyday situations.
- Generational (see Eph. 6:1-4): The Old Testament ends with the promise that God "will restore the hearts of the fathers to their children, and the heart of the children to their fathers" (Mal. 4:6). This is a reference to the reconciling work of Christ. This section teaches how this is possible today because of Him.
- Marketplace (see Eph. 6:5-9): Paul uses the two farthest points in the marketplace, masters and slaves, to highlight the widest human gap. These two groups are exact opposites of each other. The apostle shows that both have the same master, Jesus; and, therefore, they are fellow spiritual slaves of Christ, bonded together by the love of their common master.

Sin: Painfully Tangible

Bridging these six gaps allows the Church to "be strong in the Lord" (Eph. 6:10). This is essential in order to be able to struggle successfully against the forces of wickedness over this world (see Eph. 6:11-12). This, in turn, results in a dramatic power encounter (see chapter 7 for more on power encounters), as the evil one begins to lose control "in the heavenly places" (Eph. 6:12) because he loses the grip he had on the six social groups listed above.

What wrestles control away from Satan is a new social entity made up of people who previously were under his dominion and formerly hated and hurt each other, but now they worship together and selflessly serve one another (see Eph. 3:10).

The marketplace gap, listed at the end of this string of gaps, and right before the command to engage the forces of wickedness, constitutes a frontier that, once settled, paves the way for the kingdom of God to be manifest in our midst. This manifestation is very important because sin is not abstract; rather, it is tangible and painful. Nowhere is this more evident than when it comes to the issue of masters and slaves. Here I am referring to the marketplace institution of slavery, which is dehumanizing no matter what form it takes or what culture it invades. The exploitation of people and the accumulation of wealth at the expense of their tears, blood and lives represent sin at its worst. Organized, systemic indifference to the suffering inflicted upon the poor is tantamount to pouring acid on an open, oozing wound.

> **What wrestles control away from Satan is a new social entity made up of people who previously were under his dominion.**

Even though we legally have no slaves in Western nations today, social inequities still persist. The divide between the haves and the have-nots is present everywhere, even in well-developed nations where it can take the more subtle form of underpaid and exploited migrant workers. This is why what I experienced in July of 1999 was so revealing. It was the event that led me to fully reexamine my understanding of the marketplace and the kingdom of God.

A NEW VIEW OF THE MARKETPLACE

Our ministry team had arrived in the city of La Plata, Argentina, with a contingent of 331 international short-term missionaries representing five continents. The local pastors welcomed us in typical Argentine fashion, with a monumental barbecue. After dessert they did something equally awesome: they stood in pairs facing each other to form a corridor. They prayed for each visitor as he or she walked through the corridor and at the end of the line the president of the ministerial association anointed each one for service in La Plata.

When we were ready to go to the places where we would be lodged for the night, I sensed the Lord trying to communicate something to me. As I focused on Him, I received unusual instructions: *Do not touch the city until you have done two things: Take a public offering in the central plaza and give it to the city.* This was peculiar because even though I had taken offerings in public before, I had never done it on behalf of a secular institution such as a city.

I ran this idea by the pastors and they all felt excited about it. They indicated that the Children's Hospital, in dire need of $8,000 worth of repairs, was the most pressing need. We agreed to meet in the main plaza the following day.

An Unusual Offering

At the appointed time, we congregated in Plaza Moreno in the heart of the city. The local pastors and 331 short-term missionaries called on the Lord to be present. Since we did not use loudspeakers, at a glance our group looked like any other on a typical Sunday in a downtown plaza. But a closer look revealed four pastors who stood in the center of the circle holding offering bags borrowed from a nearby church as we gave our offering for the city.

Looking back I cannot say that it felt like an extraordinary moment at all. On the surface, it was just a group of nationals and internationals coming forward to put money in bags—but something was afoot in the unseen world. At the end of the exercise $11,507 (U.S.) had been collected. This was great, but what was truly extraordinary was that while the offering was being given, 23 people *asked* to receive the Lord! I mean this literally. These were passersby who *asked* to be led to Christ, even though no one was preaching or passing out gospel tracts. While we were all busy with the offering, sinners were stirred and moved in unusual ways. One person came up and said, "Whatever you have, I want it. Please, give it to me." Another asked what was going on. Even before a full reply had been given, he cried out, "I want to be like you. Please, show me how."

This was most uncommon. It was like being on a lake and having a school of fish jump into the boat!

BRIDGING THE MARKETPLACE GAP AS THE NORM

Later, when I asked the Lord about this unusual and unprecedented event, He indicated that it was neither unusual nor without precedent. It had happened before and it should happen more often. He pointed to four instances in the book of Acts where wealthy people in the Church shared their lives and resources with the poor, and in each case significant numbers of believers were spontaneously added to the Kingdom.

The first example is found in Acts 2:44-47:

> And all those who had believed were together, and had all things in common; And they began selling their property and possessions, and were sharing them with all, as anyone might have need. And day by day continuing with one mind in the temple, and breaking bread from house to house, they were taking their meals together with gladness and sincerity of heart.... And the Lord was adding to their number day by day those who were being saved.

This is the first description of Church life in the New Testament, and taking care of the needy was at its very center. Actually, it involved much more than rich people giving money to the poor. Rich and poor became amalgamated into a new social group where there were no needy people and everybody experienced gladness. The cause-and-effect relationship between joyfully and generously sharing with those in need and the daily increase in the numbers of disciples is impossible to miss.

The second example is in Acts 4:32-35:

> And the congregation of those who believed were of one heart and soul; and not one of them claimed that anything belonging to him of his own; but all things were common property to them.... for all who were owners of land or houses would sell them and bring

the proceeds of the sales and lay them at the apostles' feet, and they would be distributed to each as any had need.

Luke, before indicating that the Church also grew as a result of joyful and generous transfer of wealth, establishes a contrast. First, he highlights the exemplary behavior of Joseph, also known as Barnabas, "who owned a tract of land, sold it and brought the money and laid it at the apostles feet" (Acts 4:37). Luke then writes about the bad example of Ananias and Sapphira (see Acts 5:1-10), who brought only a portion of the sale price while pretending to have brought more. As a result this couple was struck dead, and immediately after that we read that "multitudes of men and women . . . were constantly added to their number" (Acts 5:14). Here we see again the cause-and-effect relationship between helping the poor and large numbers of people getting saved.

Understanding Why Ananias and Sapphira Dropped Dead

When we read the story of Ananias and Sapphira, there is a question that begs for an answer: Why was God so severe with them? If anyone who has failed to deliver on a promise to God were to be struck dead, very few people would be alive.

The reason for the severity was that Ananias and Sapphira were about to contaminate the pristine stream of reconciliation between rich and poor that had emerged as a core value of Christianity and that was resulting in large numbers of conversions. Taking care of the needy with gladness and sincerity of heart constituted a tangible manifestation of grace in the marketplace. In addition, as soon as the sixth of the social gaps—the marketplace gap—is bridged, the Church attains a position from which it can wrestle spiritual control away from Satan and his wicked forces. When the captors are defeated, the captives (sinners) are set free, producing a bountiful flow of new converts. Interfering with this dynamic process was (and is) no small sin.

This unfortunate couple tried to use wealth to advantageously position themselves before others, specifically Church leaders. Peter made it clear that they did not have to sell their property—even after they had sold it, the money was still theirs to use as they pleased. There was nothing wrong with holding on to the property. The evil deed was in trying to contaminate the flow of grace with a lie, and for that they were struck dead.

Leaders of an Incipient Revolt

Part of the severity of the punishment also had to do with the fact that Ananias and Sapphira appear to have been the leaders of a destructive movement emerging *within* the Church. We read that after they dropped dead, "great fear came upon the whole church . . . and they were all with one accord . . . *but none of the rest dared associate with them*, however the people held them in great esteem" (Acts 5:11-13, emphasis added). Three groups are identified in this section: the Church, the unbelievers and those referred to as "the rest." Who are they? Most likely they were members of Ananias's and Sapphira's group; therefore, fear kept them at a distance. It seems that God took very seriously any threat to the flow of reconciliation in the marketplace, as we will see again with the untimely death of Herod.

Widows, Bread and Church Growth

The third instance, which I have already noted in a previous chapter, is found in Acts 6:1-7. Here again the issue evolves around taking care of the needy: "A complaint arose on the part of the Hellenistic Jews against the native Hebrews, because their widows were being overlooked in the daily serving of food" (Acts 6:1).

To deal with the problem the apostles, as I have noted, directed that men of good reputation and full of the Spirit and of wisdom be selected to solve it. Seven men were found that met this criterion and were brought before the apostles, who prayed and laid hands on them. The moment they were placed in authority, *the number of disciples continued to increase greatly in Jerusalem* to the point that even many of the priests became obedient to the faith (see Acts 6:6). Here again we see how taking care of a marketplace inequity affecting needy widows produced immediate Church growth.

The Reason Herod Died

The fourth instance is recorded in Acts 11:26–12:25. This section begins with a prophecy given in Antioch about a great hunger that would come to Judea. The local saints took a generous offering and sent it to Judea in the hands of Paul and Barnabas. As we move into the next chapter we learn how Herod martyred James, yet an angelic intervention spared Peter. Next we read that Herod was struck dead. This sounds familiar, doesn't it? Why did God strike another person dead?

According to the Bible, it was because Herod "did not give God the glory" (Acts 12:23). This is not uncommon behavior among rulers, but what made this sin lethal was that Herod used food as a weapon while a famine was going on. He did this out of anger toward the people of Tyre and Sidon "because their country was fed by [Herod's] territory" (Acts 12:20). It is reported that right after Herod dropped dead, Paul and Barnabas, having fulfilled their charitable mission to feed the poor, returned to Antioch and "the word of the Lord continued to grow, and to be multiplied" (Acts 12:24). While many lessons can be drawn from this episode, once again we see the cause-and-effect dynamic between taking care of the poor and spontaneous evangelism.

Why would Church growth happen as a result of feeding the hungry and sharing with the needy? As I noted earlier, sin is not abstract; rather, it is tangible, particularly when people are hopelessly hungry. Whoever solves the systemic iniquity represented by this problem in our cities will remove the ugliest social wound ever carved with the serrated knife of sin. As a result they will command the respect and the attention of everybody, especially those in authority. If the Church does it, there will be an impact on the marketplace, and this in turn will have an impact on the city.

Feeding the hungry alone does not produce church growth, because hunger is a symptom, not a cause. Today there are communities where there are no hungry people but no evidence of church growth either. The Early Church did more than simply address the problem of systemic hunger. It went to the root of the problem, which is the lack of love for the needy on the part of the rich and the resulting resentment among the poor. When both the rich and the poor enter the kingdom of God, mutual hatred and contempt are replaced by fervent love. By feeding the hungry, a result of this reconciliation, the early disciples dealt with the underlying cause of poverty.

This is why Jesus taught through the parable of the 10 minas (noted in chapter 5) that people such as Zacchaeus should be the norm. He spontaneously and generously reached out to the poor. When it comes to bridging the gap between the rich and the poor, the first move always belongs to the rich, because they are the ones who have the position and resources to initiate the process.

Paul the Reconciler
I asked the Lord if there was a passage in the Scriptures that taught about reconciliation between the rich and the poor. I soon discovered that there is an entire book, albeit a short one: Philemon.

We know that Philemon was wealthy because he had servants (see v. 16) and a house big enough to host a church (see v. 2) as well as Paul and possibly his associates when they came to town (see v. 22). He was also known for *having refreshed the heart of the saints* (see v. 7). "Refreshing" means, or at least includes, the giving of gifts.

Onesimus, one of Philemon's slaves, had run away. Paul met him in prison and led him to the Lord. Paul describes Onesimus as the son "I have begotten in my imprisonment" (v. 10).

An Unusual Request
In his letter to Philemon, Paul asks for something not just unusual, but also unprecedented. Unusual would have been to ask that Philemon forgive Onesimus. But Paul asked for much more. He requested that Philemon receive Onesimus as a beloved brother (see v. 16). In the cruel, rigid, class-driven world of the first century this was exceptional, to say the least.

It is very important to understand that Paul asked for something extraordinary from *both* Philemon and Onesimus. In addition to requesting that Philemon receive Onesimus as a brother and to treat him accordingly, Paul asked Onesimus to return to the master from whom he had fled. The penalty for runaway slaves ranged from severe physical punishment to death. Therefore, Paul, the reconciler, stood in the gap, embraced both men and pleaded for them to be reconciled with each other; Paul bridged the ugliest social gap of the day. While the New

Testament does not explicitly condemn slavery, this incredible letter from Paul is clearly the seed idea that eventually resulted in the abolition of slavery as an institution.

Paul's Impeccable Record

Paul's credentials as a reconciler result from his *total* identification with *both* of them. First he calls Philemon a beloved brother, a fellow worker (see v. 1) and a companion (see v. 17). He looks forward to being hosted by him (see v. 22). He then reminds Philemon, a master, that from a spiritual perspective Paul could order him to obey but chooses to make it a request (see vv. 8,19). With this approach, Paul leaves no doubt that he feels very close to Philemon.

He paints a similar picture of Onesimus by calling him his son (see v. 10) and describes him as useful (see v. 11). He tells Philemon that in Onesimus, Paul is sending him his *own heart* (see v. 12). To better appreciate this unusual level of identification with a slave, we need to remember that Onesimus had spent time in jail. In those days prisons were utterly miserable. Dirt, vermin and infections of all kinds were rampant. There were no showers, there was a complete lack of hygiene, and released inmates were not given a change of clothes. Consequently, if Onesimus had been released before Paul and had come straight out of prison, he might have looked and smelled like a wild animal. No matter what Onesimus's physical appearance was, Paul still describes him as a reflection of his own heart.

Emulating Jesus

By identifying himself fully with both the master and the slave, Paul secured the moral ground from which to address and debunk the social injustice involving masters and slaves and to facilitate reconciliation between them. He also produced a prototype of reconciliation. This is what is needed today if we are to bridge the marketplace gap: Church leaders who can truly and fully identify with both groups and for people in those groups to know that a new order is called for. Then, and only then, will we close this ugly gap. First, Jesus, being rich, became poor so that we, being poor, may become rich. Paul simply emulated Jesus.

WHAT ABOUT US TODAY?

Bridging the wealth, or marketplace, gap is beneficial because when the wealthy and the destitute are reconciled, both are enriched. The wealthy possess a significant reservoir of hope as a result of their successes in life. They can look at challenges with a significant degree of confidence, because they have conquered so many challenges themselves and also because of the resources they have developed and accumulated through the years. On the other hand, the poor cannot tackle problems on the natural level as easily because they have no record of accomplishment from which to draw hope. However, this state of material deprivation consistently leads them to the Lord and in the process increases their capacity for faith. James said it best: "Did not God choose the poor of this world to be rich in faith?" (Jas. 2:5). Conversely, the rich do not need to exercise a lot of faith for material needs, because they already have the resources. Both groups have been entrusted with complementary blessings as a result of their stations in life and can enrich each other. When the wealthy and the poor are reconciled and walk together in an atmosphere where they can minister to each other, the rich provide hope and the poor impart faith. When faith and hope come together, love soon becomes evident (see 1 Cor. 13:13).

When the wealthy and the poor walk together, the rich provide hope and the poor impart faith.

This is why it is so important that we learn from Paul the ways we can bridge this gap. Paul and the other apostles considered caring for the poor one of their required duties (see Gal. 2:10).

Former president of the United States Jimmy Carter is a prime example of this kind of marketplace reconciliation. After having held the most powerful office on Earth, he now travels around the world building homes for poor people as a volunteer with Habitat for Humanity. However, he does not do it by just raising money, something he could easily and comfortably do given his high visibility and credibility. Instead, he builds houses alongside the future occupants, who are all extremely poor. In the process he becomes intimately acquainted with them and they get to know him, thus breaking down the wall between the rich and the poor. It is such a refreshing picture to see Jimmy Carter express the love of God this way. He embodies what Saint Francis exhorted, "Preach the gospel at all times. Use words only when necessary."

Choose a Financial Ceiling

If you are a marketplace Christian, I suggest you take the first few steps immediately, even if your efforts are at a very basic level. I suggest that you establish a ceiling as to how much money you wish to live on. Pick a figure that is comfortable because you can always reduce it. Be generous because God is not stingy, nor does He condemn wealth, as we saw in chapter 5.

Once you have chosen a figure with which you feel comfortable, make a decision that every penny over that ceiling will be given to the needy. I suggest you give it to someone who has no possibility of repaying the gift or even thanking you properly. As you move in obedience, two things will happen: The amount of money you make over your chosen ceiling will increase, thus allowing you to give even more to the needy; and you will be prompted to lower the ceiling as you experience the joy of increased giving and you will personally benefit from new divine sources of provision that result from your generosity to the poor. However, the greatest satisfaction will be seeing sinners come to the saving knowledge of Jesus when your obedience has brought the kingdom of God to them.

Poverty of the Spirit

The worst poverty is the poverty of spirit. It manifests itself when people feel, or are made to feel, inferior and, as a result, they end up confined inside spiritual ghettos. These people need to be set free. To deal with this, you need to go beyond simply giving money away. I suggest that you reach out to Christians in your circle of influence who are poorer or have a lower social standing than you do. It can be an employee, a maid or a neighbor. Reach out and affirm him or her as a brother or sister in Christ. Make it your lifestyle to pray and worship with him or her. Speak into his or her life and *let him or her speak into yours.* Allow the unbelieving world to see *how much Christians of different social positions love each other.* Bonding with people different from ourselves addresses the spiritual dimension of the problem.

But do not stop there. If you are an employer, make it your responsibility to enable your employees to live debt-free. Help them pay off their credit card debts and eventually their house mortgages. Also help them buy stock; in fact, give them bonuses so that they can afford to buy their own. You can never help them enough, because the more you help them, the more God will entrust to you. The reason for this is a very simple one: The Body of Christ always grows proportionally. God will not allow one arm to be twice as long as the other. In the Body of Christ we are members of one another. How much God entrusts to you is determined by the position of the neediest Christian in your sphere of influence. As you raise that person up, you will also raise your own ceiling. Remember, God wants to see His kingdom evidenced in your sphere of influence. As you show faithfulness in little things, God will avail you of greater opportunities, because He is actively looking for people who will bridge the marketplace gap.

The Path to Reconciliation in the Marketplace

In Ephesians we have a clear picture of the reconciliation continuum that God has designed for the marketplace. Paul writes,

> Be angry, and yet do not sin; do not let the sun go down on your anger, and do not give the devil an opportunity. Let him who steals steal no longer; but rather let him labor, performing with his own hands what is good, in order that he might have something to share with him who has need. Let no unwholesome word proceed from your mouth, but only such a word as is good for edification according to the need of the moment, that it may give grace to those who hear. And do not grieve the Holy Spirit, by whom you were sealed for the day of redemption (Eph. 4:26-30).

This passage presents God's strategy to change a thief into a benefactor and a grabber into a giver. The thief must first stop stealing and then begin to work *with his own hands*, become self-reliant and prosper so that he is able to give to others. In the natural, this deals a decisive blow to crime in society. However, the spiritual picture is even more dramatic. It shows the transformation journey of a *destructive* person who was once under Satan's jurisdiction but has come under the control of the Holy Spirit and is now *edifying* others. What a transformation!

When enough people are swept into this transformation continuum, the city is changed. When sinners are set free from the control of the devil, they cease to be controlled by sin, are filled with the Holy Spirit and begin to help others; and the kingdom of God becomes evident.

A dramatic contemporary example is found in the city of Almolonga, Guatemala. More than 90 percent of its population is Christian. All of the bars and the jail have closed—for good. Crime is nonexistent. Almolonga, an agrarian community, produces phenomenal crops and ships them all over Central America. Poverty and unemployment have been eradicated. This extraordinary story has been extensively documented in numerous books and in the *Transformation* video. However, the point that should not be missed is that the Almolonga revival *is a marketplace revival*.

Almolonga is a living example of 2 Chronicles 7:14. If we picture it as a triangle, on one side we will see God's people repenting for their sins. On the second side is God's response of forgiveness. And on the third side, the land is healed. The healing of the land not only resulted in extraordinary conversions—90 percent of the population—but also in turning formerly arid land into fields that produce the richest of harvests. As if to leave no doubt that such prosperity is the result of God's blessing, the earth's extraordinary fertility stops right on the border of the city.

Almolonga should not be the exception; rather, it should be the norm. Can you picture for a moment what could happen if the same revival were to take place on Wall Street, in Silicon Valley or in Asia's new markets? The principles are universal. God is the same. Similar sins are waiting to be forgiven and the land is waiting to be healed. Will you begin the process in your marketplace?

The Church is God's vehicle to bring His kingdom to the city, as we will see in the next chapter.

CHAPTER 7

THE KINGDOM, THE CHURCH AND THE MARKETPLACE

People often talk about the sacred-secular divide, but my faith tells me that God is found in earth and rocks and buildings and institutions, and, yes, in the business world.

DAVID MILLER, FORMER IBM EXECUTIVE

The kingdom of God, the central theme of Jesus' teachings, was all over the place in His time. He referred to the kingdom of God, or the kingdom of heaven, 78 times. His examples consistently indicate that God's kingdom comes near people to make it possible for them to come into it *while they are on Earth* (see Luke 10:9; 16:16). The idea that Jesus only talked about transferring people to heaven when He mentioned the Kingdom is not correct. In fact, the opposite is true.

He compared the Kingdom to seeds, light, salt, deliverance from demons, healing of the sick, helping the poor and loving neighbors (see Matt. 9:35; 12:28; 13:24,33; Luke 10:7-9). His examples had to do with life on Earth as much as or more than with life in heaven. He brought the kingdom of God with Him wherever He went.

This was not something limited exclusively to Jesus. He instructed *us* to pray that God's kingdom would come and that His will would be done on Earth as it is done in heaven (see Luke 11:2-4). Let us pause for a moment to grasp the revolutionary nature of this statement. We know that the will of God is done in heaven. Whatever God desires, it happens. But the object of this prayer is for *the same thing* to happen on Earth; that is, that the will of God will be enforced down here.

This prayer was not meant to express an abstract desire, because Jesus gave specific instructions on how to go about bringing God's kingdom to Earth (see Luke 10:2-9). His parting words, as recorded by Mark, indicate that we should expect to see miracles similar to the ones He performed (see Mark 16:15-18)—and even greater ones (see John 14:12-14). Paul described the assignment he received from the Lord as opening the eyes of sinners for them to turn from darkness to light, from the dominion of Satan to God, in order to receive forgiveness of sins and an inheritance in a holy community (see Acts 26:18). These New Testament passages describe actions aimed at wresting control from Satan in order to set captives free and for the will of God to be done on Earth *as it is done in heaven.* This is intended to transform not just individuals, but *also* the environment and the conditions around them. Unfortunately we have been deceived into believing that the kingdom of God and all it brings belong in the past or in the future but not in the present.[1]

THE HEART OF THE DECEPTION

The heart of Satan's deception has to do with our understanding of the kingdom of God, the nature of the Church and the Church's role in the marketplace. We have been led to believe

- the kingdom of God is something that will manifest itself exclusively in the future, on the other side of the rapture;
- the Church is supposed to be confined to a building;
- the marketplace is the bunker of the devil and has to be avoided at all costs.

These and other deceptions have driven us into a reactionary position. Since the devil cannot extinguish the light of God in us, he has tricked us into hiding it under the pews. What a contrast to what we see in Jesus, who always presented the Kingdom, the Church and the marketplace as thoroughly integrated and interactive.

The Here and Now

These deceptions have, in turn, produced a perception of the Kingdom that misses its most important tense: *the present tense.* We have no doubt that the Kingdom existed *yesterday.* We also look forward to the Kingdom that is coming *tomorrow,* but we do not believe in the kingdom of God for *today.* This has reduced marketplace Christians to living in a concentration camp without the hope of ever taking it over. Believers are reduced to enduring with dignity the indignities imposed upon them by the enemy in control of the camp (marketplace). Our credo has become, "God's kingdom will come, either by death or by the rapture, but in the meantime all we can do is endure as gallantly as possible with no hope of God's will ever being done on Earth as it is done in heaven."

What a terrible way to live!

The Apostles' View of the Kingdom

The Church, as cited in Acts, did not hold such a dour outlook on the Kingdom and the marketplace. Rather, the concept of the kingdom of God on Earth was normative when the epistles were written. Paul defined it as "righteousness and peace and joy in the Holy Spirit" (Rom. 14:17). The tendency today is to view righteousness, peace and joy exclusively on a vertical plane between God and us. However, in this passage Paul describes horizontal—human to human—righteousness: "Do not let what is for you a good thing be spoken of as evil [by others]" (Rom. 14:16). Paul takes the same approach with peace: "Pursue the things which make for peace and the building up of one another" (Rom. 14:19). And he does likewise with joy: "It is good not to . . . do anything by which your brother stumbles. Happy is he who does not condemn himself in what he approves" (Rom. 14:21-22).

All these references and applications to the horizontal dimension of life confirm that the Early Church saw the kingdom of God as something tangible that had a deep effect on interpersonal relationships. This happened when Christians related to one another and to the lost in a context where the will of God was done on Earth. In such an environment righteousness, peace and joy became the norm, rather than the exception.

A Major Paradigm Shift

Jesus' ministry on Earth caused a major paradigm shift and changed people's understanding of the kingdom of God. Jesus referred to God's kingdom as present (see Matt. 12:28), imminent (see Mark 9:1) and in the future (see Matt. 26:29; Mark 14:25). In His day, some people embraced and entered into this new understanding (see Matt. 21:31); others fell short (see Matt. 19:24). To an audience accustomed to seeing the Temple as the place where God manifested Himself, the level of immediacy between God and the people who embraced His kingdom was exciting but very difficult to grasp.

Starting in Jerusalem

The difficulty in understanding this new perspective is why the disciples—during their last corporate interaction with Jesus—had hoped for a restoration of the Kingdom to Israel (see Acts 1:6). Such an outcome would have once again made Jerusalem and the Temple the epicenter of God's activity on Earth. Instead Jesus specified that God's move would involve Jerusalem as the staging ground, but it would spread out toward the ends of the earth (see Acts 1:8).

The First Conversions

Consistent with this, the first batch of converts—3,000 men—was harvested in an open-air meeting, rather than inside a religious building. This departure from what was expected gave birth to a movement. Since God did not want it to be confined to the Temple, much less to the synagogue, a mystery was revealed: the Church. This is a concept for which there was no existing paradigm, but it soon spread all over the city (see Acts 5:28).

The Church and the Church Building

Unfortunately, 2,000 years later, even though we know a lot about the church—how to plant and grow one—we do not know much about the kingdom of God. The Church has replaced the kingdom of God in our dispensational thinking. Worse yet, our focus is now on bringing people into the church *building* instead of taking the kingdom of God *to* where the people are.

This has resulted in a Church that is confined and centripetal rather than dynamic and expansive like the Kingdom of which Jesus spoke. The Church that began as a movement has become a monument. The roots of this misbelief go right back to the belief we have been taught, that the Church was born in the Upper Room, inside four walls. This is not true. The Church was born on the streets the day Peter preached the first sermon and thousands of people acknowledged Jesus as Messiah.

> **As long as we believe that the Church was born between four walls, we will always need four walls to have a church.**

Taking Church Outside the Walls

As long as we believe that the Church was born between four walls, we will always need four walls to have a church, a concept that will lead us to confuse the church *building* with the Church, the *ekklesia*. This misconception becomes ingrained in parishioners' minds as they are exhorted *to come to church.* And when we say that we are equating the church *building* with the Church itself, it further legitimizes the deception. Instead of having Church all over the city (see Acts 2:42), most of our energy and resources end up being devoted to acquiring and maintaining a venue where believers congregate a few times a week. This, in turn, reduces church to a couple of hours on Sunday inside a building and leaves the other 165 or so hours in the week to be lived *outside* of it. What a contrast with life in the Early Church! First-century Christians had church every day, several times a day: "They were continually devoting themselves to the apostles teaching and to fellowship, to the breaking of bread and to prayer" (Acts 2:42). They congregated even during mealtimes (see Acts 2:46)!

Not an Enemy

When church is identified primarily with a building, it soon turns centripetal in its focus and everything on the outside becomes adversarial, turning the city and the marketplace into enemies that have to be subdued, destroyed or avoided. This leads to a state of animosity, if not of all-out war, against the city and its central components: business, education and government. This attitude has produced a spiritual-ghetto mentality that isolates us from the people to whom we are called to bring the salvation message. Ghetto dwellers possess certain common characteristics. They believe they are so unique that they must remain separated from others and they are convinced they are superior, but they are also extremely insecure about interacting with anyone they consider inferior. These traits are also found in churches that have developed ghetto mentalities.

An Agency of Heaven

When Jesus introduced the notion of the Church, He linked it to the kingdom of heaven, presenting the Kingdom and the Church as two sides of the same coin. On this momentous occasion He said to Peter, "You are Peter, and upon this rock I will build My church; and the gates of Hades will not overpower it. I will give you the keys of the kingdom of heaven; and *whatever you bind on earth shall have been bound in heaven, and whatever you loose on earth shall have been loosed in heaven*" (Matt. 16:18-19, emphasis added).

In this quote in Matthew, Jesus clearly stated that His Church would overpower the kingdom of darkness. He went on to explain that to accomplish this, the keys of the kingdom of heaven would be made available to believers so that the will of God could happen on Earth. To emphasize the human component, the Lord said that Peter would get the keys, obviously as a forerunner of every church member. Nowadays we do not have a problem believing that something ethereal like the Church has power over the kingdom of evil. But Jesus explicitly spoke to one person, Peter, and told him that spiritual keys would be given to him in order to change things on Earth. The Lord Jesus never put the kingdom of God and the Church in separate dispensations or locations.

Bringing the Kingdom of God to Earth

The Church exists to bring the kingdom of God to Earth. We know that this is true because on two occasions that Jesus discussed the Church (see Matt. 16:18; 18:17), He also referred to the fact that . . . *whatever you bind on earth shall have been bound in heaven, and whatever you loose on earth shall have been loosed in heaven* . . . Obviously this is a Body entrusted with authority.

The reference to binding and releasing on Earth for a corresponding action to happen in heaven poses an interesting question: How much can the Church affect what goes on in heaven? Obviously, the heaven Jesus spoke of cannot be God's heaven, since He is sovereign and almighty. He cannot be affected, much less bound, by any action initiated by humans on Earth, His Church included. Consequently, it has to be the heavenly places where Satan and his forces of wickedness have established their dominion. Paul described it vividly when he wrote, "For our struggle is . . . against the rulers, against the powers, against the world forces of this darkness, against the spiritual forces of wickedness *in the heavenly places*" (see Eph. 6:12, emphasis added).

It follows that the Church has been entrusted with authority and power to struggle effectively against this evil empire. The struggle cannot be for the personal salvation of its members, since the devil cannot take us away from Jesus' hand. It cannot be about sanctification, because that is the work of the Holy Spirit. Basically it has to be about seeing

God's will established where satanic activity and schemes are actively challenging it. Paul spoke of this type of power when he stated that his assignment was to open the eyes of sinners so that they will turn from the *dominion* of Satan to God's *kingdom* (see Acts 26:18). There are two kingdoms at war with each other, and the Church is God's agency to advance His kingdom on Earth. For this purpose it has been entrusted with authority.

In fact, the Greek word for church, ekklesia, was widely used in the Roman Empire. It is used three times in a secular context in the book of Acts (see 19:30-42), but the translators chose to render it as "assembly." The purpose for this gathering (ekklesia) was to obtain legal action against Paul—in this case the silversmiths were concerned that Paul was ruining their business by preaching against idols. They wanted to bind Paul.

Jesus presented the Church as an assembly of His followers that had the power to advocate the will of God on Earth. In fact, in the first sermon of the Church age, Peter stated that the gospel must be preached until all things are placed under the feet of Jesus (see Acts 2:34-35). At that moment the will of God will indeed be fully done *on Earth* as it is done in heaven. However, we tend to overlook the progressive dimension that indicates that the will of God will be done on Earth in increments until such fullness is achieved. This misunderstanding leads us to believe that the fullness will happen at the very end of time on Earth, when the Lord returns and that, in the meantime, this world is bound to remain under the control of the evil one, unaffected by the Church. This passivity on our part has no biblical foundation.

When Jesus introduced the concept of the Church, He stated that the gates of hell would not prevail against it. Gates are not offensive weapons. They are defensive in nature and function. Therefore, the gates of hell cannot attack the Church. It is the other way around. Hence the promise of victory when the Church storms the gates of hell. Of course, the Lord will win the ultimate victory Himself. At that time, His kingdom will be established forever. But until such a time comes, the Church is empowered and commissioned by the Lord to storm the gates of hell.

The Church in the Whole World

The Church in the New Testament stormed the gates of hell, and the Church is always presented as victorious—not even once is it seen as weak or defeated. The standard for what to do on Earth is God's order in heaven: "Thy will be done, in earth, as it is in heaven" (Matt. 6:10, *KJV*). This command was never rescinded.

In fact, in Acts, in the Epistles and in Revelation, the Church is consistently described in relationship to cities, such as the church at Antioch or at Jerusalem. This is true because in the same fashion that Jesus brought the kingdom of God to those He came in contact with, the Early Church brought it to cities, regions and nations. When I refer to the Church, I mean *the people* that constitute the congregation, not a building or institution. The Church is men and women, masters and slaves, parents and children who have been set free from the kingdom of darkness and transferred to the kingdom of light. These people carried that Kingdom with them wherever they went.

Church Planting and the Bible

The disciples knew that they were to witness all over the city, and when they did, a *church was planted.* They never saw themselves as establishing an outpost of heaven inside a building called church in the midst of a city they did not believe could be reached or transformed. To the contrary, they saw themselves infiltrating the fiber of the city. Their model was salt and light, elements that touch, penetrate and change that with which they come in contact (see Matt. 5:13,16).

Why Paul Goes into the Marketplace

As we have already seen in an earlier chapter, when Paul, a rabbi, joined the Church, he naturally gravitated toward the synagogue in his initial evangelistic endeavors, making synagogue-preaching his main focus. But after repeated rejection he announced that he was moving on to the Gentiles (see Acts 13:46). Even though Paul, upon arriving in a city, always went to a synagogue, if there was one, he began to gravitate more and more toward the Gentiles. This happened so often that by the time he arrived in Corinth (see Acts 18:1-9), he deliberately *exchanged* the synagogue for a private home.

This allowed him to teach and preach *every day*, instead of only on the Sabbath. Obviously, Gentiles did not meet in synagogues; they gathered in public forums, business places and plazas—in the marketplace. Paul, like Peter, John, James and Philip, turned those public forums into places where the presence and the power of God became evident to the lost in the city.

In short, the kingdom of God was manifested where common folks gathered, just like in Jesus' day, except that it quickly transcended the familiar territory of Judea and Samaria. As the disciples moved deeper into Gentile territory, the marketplace became central to the Church's activities, especially evangelistic endeavors.

Why Violence Is Necessary

Jesus indicated that the kingdom of heaven suffers violence and that violent people will take it by force (see Matt. 11:12). Why is force necessary? Because establishing God's kingdom on Earth requires confronting the kingdom of darkness.

This is a process that always begins in the individual but needs to keep expanding. At first a power encounter causes the sinner to surrender to Jesus. As the presence of God floods his or her soul, the works of the devil are destroyed and a new order is established. But God's design does not stop at the outer limit of His children's skin. His plan is for the same transformation to happen in their circle of influence. First in the family, next in the neighborhood and eventually all over the city.

Ephesus is a classic example. Paul and his apostolic band taught the Word of God to multitudes of disciples for two years, and then a power encounter took place. Large numbers of witches and warlocks were saved. They publicly burnt their demonic paraphernalia. This was accompanied by extraordinary miracles. As a result, all of the people who lived in the Roman province of Asia heard the Word of the Lord (see Acts 19:10). This is just one example. As the disciples spread the gospel, they often saw power encounters.

Power Encounters and Divine Intervention

Acts records 40 major supernatural actions, many of which are dramatic power encounters. It is interesting that only one of them took place in a religious setting: the healing of the lame man at the Temple gate called Beautiful (see Acts 3:1-10). This highlights the fact that the Early Church was not confined to a building or to a prearranged schedule of meetings. In Acts, the Church was a movement that shook or took cities. The 39 supernatural actions that took place in the marketplace are listed below.

Divine Interventions from the Book of Acts

Here are the 39 major divine interventions, or supernatural events, that happened in the marketplace or nearby. This roster from Acts is quite impressive.

Acts Reference	Divine Interventions	Location
2:37-41	Three-thousand men were pierced to the heart by Peter's preaching and were then baptized.	City streets
4:30-31	An earthquake served as an echo for God's amen to the disciples' first recorded corporate prayer.	Believers' gathering
5:12-14	There were signs, wonders and salvation for many at Solomon's Portico.	Public square
5:15-16	Streets turned into healing venues.	City streets
5:19	An angel set Peter free from prison.	Prison
7:56	Stephen received a celestial vision.	City streets
8:5-8,13	Philip performed signs and wonders, cast out demons and healed the sick, bringing much rejoicing to Samaria.	City streets
8:18-24	Peter had a power encounter with a magician.	City streets
8:26	An angel gave directions to Phillip.	City streets
8:39	Supernatural transportation was provided for Phillip.	Desert road
9:1-9	Jesus appeared to Saul of Tarsus on a public road. The Lord spoke in a vision to Ananias.	Damascas road

Acts Reference	Divine Interventions	Location
9:10-16	The Lord spoke in a vision to Ananias.	Home
9:18	Scales fell off the eyes of Paul upon receiving the Holy Spirit.	Home
9:32-35	The entire population of Lydda and Sharon turned to the Lord as a result of Peter healing Aeneas.	City streets
9:40-43	Dorcas was raised from the dead and many people in Joppa believed in Jesus.	Home
10:1-6	The vision of an angel was given to Cornelius.	Home
10:9-16	Peter fell into a trance while praying in the home of Simon, a businessman, and received specific guidance from the Lord.	Home
10:44-48	The Holy Spirit fell on God-fearing Gentiles in the home of a Roman centurion.	Gentile home
12:1-19	The hand of the Lord was with some of those who fled Jerusalem after Stephen's death, and many pagans came to the Lord for the first time. An angel delivered Peter from jail again.	Prison
12:23	An angel struck Herod dead.	Palace
13:6-12	Paul had a power encounter with a magician.	City streets
13:48-50	Great crowds assembled to hear the Word, and many Gentiles believed as the gospel spread over an entire region.	City streets
14:1-5	Signs and wonders were performed to validate the message of the Apostles.	City streets
14:8-11	A lame man was healed in public in Lystra.	City streets
16:9-10	A vision was given to Paul.	Home
16:16-18	A power encounter occurred in the marketplace; it resulted in the deliverance of a slave girl from a divining spirit.	Public square

Acts Reference	Divine Interventions	Location
16:26	An earthquake set Paul and Silas free from prison and led to the salvation of the jailer and his family.	Prison
17:5-9	Wicked men of the marketplace failed to kill the apostles.	City streets
17:17	Paul turned the marketplace into a classroom.	Public square
19:10	Paul turned a school owned by Tyrannus into a staging ground to saturate Asia with the gospel in the next two years.	Lecture hall
19:11-13	Extraordinary miracles were performed by Paul.	City streets
19:17	Jewish exorcists were publicly put to shame by demons.	City streets
19:18-20	Many magicians got saved and afterwards burned their demonic paraphernalia.	Public square
19:23-41	A marketplace rebellion orchestrated by Demetrius and his union was foiled.	Public square
20:6-12	A young man was raised from the dead	Home
23:11	The Lord appeared by Paul's side inside the Roman barracks, and comforted him.	Prison
27:23-26	An angel delivered a message to Paul who preached it on the deck of a ship.	Ship
28:1-5	Paul overcame the bite of a viper.	Beach
28:8-10	A nobleman was healed, followed by many others from all over Malta.	Home

Make the Boardroom Your Pulpit

We can expect God to show up in the marketplace. This is why today the boardroom should be to those anointed to serve in the marketplace what the pulpit is to pastors, and the people in their sphere of influence what the congregation is to an ordained minister. The notion that the marketplace is less spiritual than a church is false.

Case Study: A Bar Becomes a Church

The story of Joe, a jeepney (taxi) owner and driver in the Philippines, provides a vivid illustration of the way the kingdom of God, the Church and the marketplace can interact to transform individuals and touch a city.

As Joe was driving his jeepney shortly after his conversion to Christianity, he heard God tell him to serve right where he was. Since he was a new believer and the marketplace was what he knew best, he focused on a bar called Sweet Moments. He decided to apply the principles of prayer evangelism as listed in Luke 10 to make peace with the lost, fellowship with them, take care of them and eventually announce that the kingdom of God has come near them (see Luke 10:1-8).

> The boardroom should be to those anointed to serve in the marketplace what the pulpit is to pastors.

Every day he would go into the bar, order a soft drink and pray peace over the place, its employees and the customers. After a few days of doing this, he befriended the manager, Brian, who was a homosexual, a gambler, a drug user, a drug dealer and a pimp to 35 prostitutes. This pedigree left no doubt that Brian was a certified, full-strength sinner.

The friendship grew. After just a few days Joe was able to lead Brian to the Lord and baptize him at a nearby beach. As Brian emerged from the water, the power of God came upon him and he experienced an instant transformation. All of his homosexual drives disappeared. He was also freed from gambling and drug addiction. He was delivered from all of the vices and stopped being a pimp, which had supported his sinful lifestyle.

Brian's transformation became evident to those around him, and in a very short time all 35 prostitutes also became Christians. Joe and his wife decided to move into a neighborhood near the bar so that they could minister to this unusual congregation. His wife baked rice cakes, prayed over them and distributed them among their neighbors, using food as way of introduction. One of those neighbors was Teddy, a lawyer who was also the owner of the bar. He later testified that when he ate one of those cakes something happened to him. He became interested in what Joe had been teaching his employees, joined the Bible study and soon became a Christian. As he grew in the Lord, he realized that his line of business was not pleasing to God and turned the bar into a church. In less than a year Joe, the pastor of the bar-turned-church, established 12 cell groups in the area, and the kingdom of God has come to a significant portion of the marketplace.

The key? Joe saw the church as the means to take the kingdom of God to people in the marketplace. When sinners discovered that the Kingdom had come near them, they came into it; and once they did, he simply taught them how to have church in the marketplace!

God, Money and Mammon

A major obstacle that prevents church from happening in the marketplace is the fear that the church will become corrupt if it comes in contact with money, the bloodline of business. Jesus lashed out at the moneychangers in the Temple courts, and this seems to add credence to this concern. However, the moneychangers were thieves preying on the faith of the people. Every time people use money for personal gain at the expense of God's kingdom, they incur God's wrath. This is true whether it happens in church settings or in the marketplace. The fact that many ministers have mismanaged or misappropriated church funds is deplorable. However, no one is suggesting that churches stop taking offerings because of it. The issue is not the money but how to handle it. As I indicated in earlier chapters, Jesus as well as His disciples were skilled at handling resources. There is a right way and a wrong way.

Bishop Vaughn McLaughlin, in Jacksonville, Florida, has found the right way. The Potter's House, a congregation of 3,000 members he leads, was instrumental in purchasing a 42,000-square-foot building. But instead of devoting it mainly to church meetings on Sundays, as most churches do, McLaughlin decided to impact the community. The building now houses 21 businesses, including a bus terminal, financial planning service, law practice and recording studio. According to an article written by Adrienne S. Gaines and published in *Charisma*, the refurbished facility "has served as an incubator for entrepreneurs within the church and broader community. The Potter's House covers all overhead costs; the tenants give back to the ministry as their businesses prosper, never fearing eviction."[2]

The Potter's House also runs a credit union and a school for 500 students who pay very low tuition. It has also provided funding for a community youth basketball project. Even though Bishop McLaughlin is in full-time ministry, he has also entered the marketplace by personally purchasing a facility that offers the same opportunity to 14 additional businesses.

According to *Charisma*, the strategy seems to be working in Jacksonville. What used to be a dilapidated and hard-hit community has been infused with new life. Many national chains have opened shops in the area, and thousands of lives have been changed.

Bishop McLaughlin summarized his vision: "We were thinking community. How can we get this community serviced and into this facility to hear the gospel? This was the whole purpose of the Multiplex. Our goal was to transform this community."[3] It appears that he has developed a good model of how to correctly handle money. Anyone who visits the Potter's House will know that church is taking place in the marketplace and that the kingdom of God is in evidence by the transformation in lives as well as in the community.

Notes

1. A detailed explanation of prayer evangelism can be found in my book *Prayer Evangelism* (Ventura, CA: Regal Books, 2000).
2. Adrienne S. Gaines, "The Church That Changed a City," *Charisma* (October 2001), p. 50.
3. Ibid.

CHAPTER 8

GOD IN THE
BOARDROOM

God is looking for men and women who will allow their "staffs" and "donkeys" to be used to perform miracles. Will you allow Him to use yours?

OS HILLMAN, FAITH AND WORK

The Church is the light of the world and its members are the salt of the earth, but the marketplace is the heart of the city. To take a city or a nation, short of war, requires conquering its markets, since whoever is in charge of them will run the city. Looking at it another way, it can be said that the captains of industry are the city's secular elders.

The skyline of a city defines its identity the way physical appearance identifies humans. Today skylines consist not so much of church spires, but of the buildings that house the corporations that breathe life into commercial arteries. It is right there where the kingdom of God needs to be established. Those are the corporations that must experience the power and the presence of God. For a city to be transformed, complete change has to come to the marketplace, and Christian businesspeople must play a key role.

What exactly is that role? The role is always determined by the kind of relationship Christians have with the marketplace. The four levels are

1. to be a Christian in the marketplace,
2. to be a Christian who applies biblical principles in the marketplace,
3. to be a Christian who does business in the fullness and in the power of the Holy Spirit, and
4. to be a Christian committed to the total transformation of the marketplace.

On the first level are those who believe the marketplace is an evil place but feel they can hold their ground as Christians. Survival is their objective, and they need a lot of maintenance because they see themselves as POWs, forced to survive with dignity in an undignified place.

The second level represents those who apply Christian principles in the marketplace. They have a more positive outlook than those on level one but do not believe that applying Christian principles can do much for the corporation where they work, much less for the marketplace as a whole. Those principles allow them to overcome temptations and to keep a good testimony. Basically they settled for a draw: They will not change the marketplace and the marketplace will not change them.

On the third level we find Christians who wholeheartedly believe that they can work in the fullness of the power of the Holy Spirit. They seek God every day, they hear from Him, and they implement what He tells them.

The fourth level represents those who, after they have experienced God's transforming power in their business, see themselves on a mission to transform the marketplace.

In this chapter you will find examples that belong on the third and fourth levels.

PRAYING FOR CHRISTIANS

My friend and colleague Rick Heeren has pioneered marketplace transformation. He was trained in business and left a top-level position with Aetna Insurance Company to minister in the marketplace as part of Harvest Evangelism.

He has developed a team of businesspeople who go into boardrooms to minister to corporations in the power of the Holy Spirit. He has seen tremendous breakthroughs, which he is presently capturing in a book, *Marketplace Christian*. What follows is taken from the chapter "Praying for Christians."

Because this is a spiritual battle, we need to use spiritual weapons. Prayer and intercession are "divinely powerful weapons," which need to be included in the tool kits of every marketplace Christian.

When I first joined Ed Silvoso, he said that he sensed that I was going to develop a new ministry of praying for businesses. I have now prayed for many businesses and this chapter provides testimonies showing that prayer and intercession are good for business. Many people think that we pray just for new sales and more profits. What we have found, however, is that sin inhibits God from bringing His blessing to the company. In fact, 2 Chronicles 7:13 states that in response to sin, God is the One who stops the rain from falling on crops, causes the locusts to eat them or sends pestilence among the people.

2 Chronicles 7:14 is the antidote:

[If] My people who are called by My name humble themselves and pray, and seek My face and turn from their
wicked ways, then I will hear from heaven, will forgive
their sin, and will heal their land [company].

When God's people humble themselves and pray and repent
for their sins, they remove that which hinders God from answer-
ing prayer (2 Chron. 7:15). Consequently, "Now My eyes will be
open and My ears attentive to prayer made in this place."

Unfortunately many Sunday-only Christians operate in the
marketplace, from Monday through Friday, out of the futility of
their own thinking (Eph. 4:17). This is because they do not pray.
Marketplace Christians who pray have wisdom and revelation
knowledge from the Lord. James 4:2 teaches us that "You do not
have because you do not ask."

Now let's compare Moses with Solomon. First, in Exodus
31:1-11 we read that God was speaking to Moses in order to give
him spiritual knowledge so that he would know how to implement
the plans that God had given him for the Tabernacle. In the first
few verses, the Lord tells Moses that He has called Bezalel and that
He "has filled him with the Spirit of God, in wisdom, in understanding, in knowledge, and in all manner of workmanship."

In essence, Moses did not know how to build the Tabernacle,
so God anointed and appointed a skilled craftsman named
Bezalel to do the work.

In 2 Chronicles 2:3,7 we see something quite different:
"Then Solomon sent word to Huram the king of Tyre, saying,
'. . . Send me a man skillful to work in gold, silver, brass and iron,
and in purple, crimson and violet fabrics, and who knows how
to make engravings.'" Instead of consulting with the Lord
regarding how to build the Temple, Solomon asked a pagan king
to send him his best craftsman.

This is a good example of how many marketplace Christians are operating their companies today. They are operating in a substandard manner, because they are copying the best-demonstrated practices of non-Christian companies.

The testimonies that follow show how the Lord provided the wisdom needed to solve real-life problems in the marketplace.

Publicly Traded Company
A Christian friend called me one day. He was then a vice president of a major publicly traded company. He said that his company was losing millions of dollars and asked if I would bring a team of intercessors in order to pray and to discover why such unusually bad financial results were being experienced. Because we follow the biblical principle of submitting to those having spiritual authority over a business, my friend requested and obtained the CEO's permission to bring the intercessors into the office.

We brought about 20 intercessors into that office in downtown Minneapolis. After a substantial season of prayer, one of our team members was walking through the entryway in this company and was brought to his knees as he sensed something demonic in that area. We pulled him out of the area, and then several others went in to investigate. What we found was a waist-high pedestal with an art object on it. The sign next to the art object read that this little house on the pedestal was called "a spirit dwelling." In other words, it was a house for demons! Just what every company needs in its entryway.

This discovery was a substantial tip-off about the reason that the company was experiencing such negative financial results. As we walked around the building, we found that every single piece of art, both paintings and statues, was occult in origin. These art objects had been placed around the facility, as a form of witchcraft, in order to curse the finances of the company.

As we prayed about this, the Lord gave me a word of knowledge and directed me to the Old Testament story in 1 Samuel 5:2-4, where the Philistines captured the Ark of the Covenant and placed it in the temple of their god, named Dagon. In these verses, we see the principle of a "power encounter." By this I mean that when the presence of God is brought into direct confrontation with the presence of the demonic, the power of God always overcomes the power of the demonic. As I reflected upon this situation, the Lord impressed upon me that each of us, as Christians, is like a portable Ark of the Covenant. In other words, greater is He that is in us, than he that is in the world.

> We did not have authority to remove the demonic artwork, so we simply took spiritual authority over each object.

But now, in addition to indwelling each of us as individuals, as two or three of us gathered together in the name of Jesus Christ, the Lord was also in the midst of us (see Matt. 18:20). Ed Silvoso calls this "the presiding Jesus."[1] As we prayed in this fashion, the power of the presiding Jesus overcame the power of the witchcraft curses connected to the art objects.

We did not have authority to remove the demonic artwork, so we simply took spiritual authority over each object, and when we were finished, we left the building. A few weeks later, a newspaper headline reported that the company's financial position had suddenly turned positive.

Christian Foundation

A friend, who is a marketplace Christian, runs a Christian foundation that was created by a for-profit company many years ago. The for-profit firm had committed to give 5 percent of its pretax profit as an annual donation to the foundation. Because of the lack of profitability in the for-profit company, the foundation had not received any donations from this source in about three years. One day, my friend asked me to call a few intercessors together in order to pray on-site at the for-profit company. My friend said, "Perhaps the Holy Spirit will help us identify and eliminate the issue that is hurting their profitability."

My friend and I and about four intercessors arrived at the corporate headquarters on a Saturday night. The president and two or three board members welcomed us into the boardroom. After fellowshipping with them for a short while, I suggested that we begin to pray. As we started to pray, the Lord whispered in my ear, "Broken relationship." I stopped the prayer and asked the president if there were any broken relationships in the company.

He said, "Not now, but there was a significant one many years ago." He explained, "My predecessor, the founder of the company, had a vice president who was also his best friend. They did everything together. One day they got into a huge argument. The vice president resigned on the spot and stormed out of the president's office, never to be heard from again. That vice president went out and formed a competitor business, which has now become the number two company in our industry. Our company is the market leader in our industry."

I explained 2 Chronicles 7:14 and asked if the current president would be willing to stand in the gap and repent on behalf of his predecessor, for his part in the broken relationship. The president said that he would be willing to do it, so I asked him to kneel, as a form of humility. Then I led him in a prayer of confession, repentance and asking the Lord for forgiveness. Then I walked over to him and laid my hand on his shoulder and declared, "This sin is forgiven in the name of Jesus Christ. This iniquity is now broken off and will no longer influence this company."

Within seven days the former vice president (now competitor) called the current president and said, "I don't know why I am doing this. I just feel like we have been apart for too long. I feel like we are supposed to be together." Those two men had lunch the following week and began discussions about the idea of merging their two companies together. On May 31, 1999, those two companies merged and they now constitute the largest company in their industry. They have also gone public with an initial public offering (IPO).

One of the most exciting aspects of this deal is that the provision for 5 percent of pretax earnings to be given to my friend's Christian foundation remained intact after the merger and after the IPO.

Import Business

Another friend, who is a marketplace Christian, imports products from Korea and sells them through large operations such as Wal-Mart and Home Depot. A few years ago he was having difficulty generating sales volume. He asked me if I would pray for this "felt need." My wife, Rachel, and I went over to his home and prayed with him and his wife. After a few minutes of prayer I received a word of knowledge, the word "receivables." I stopped the prayer and asked my friend about his receivable situation. He said, "Receivables management is not a problem in our company. We monitor our receivables closely and people pay their bills on a timely basis." Then he paused, and looked very thoughtful. Then he continued, "Well, there is this one guy in another state who is way overdue in paying his bill. I have sent him threatening notes, but he has not responded."

I said, "Perhaps the Lord wants you to send this guy a note telling him that you can imagine that his problems must be very great if they keep him from paying your bill. Perhaps the Lord wants you to forgive the amount that he owes you." My friend responded immediately, "I can't run a business that way. I will never make any money if word gets around that I forgave this receivable." I responded, "Why don't you just pray about it and we'll talk later."

My wife and I left his office and returned home. A few hours later my friend called me and said, "I sent him the letter. I told him that I was writing off his receivable. I blessed him and told him that I was praying that his business problems would get solved." The next day my friend called again to tell me that he had just been awarded the largest contract in the history of his company. I asked him if he thought that there was any connection between his obedience to that word that the Lord had given us and the receipt of this new piece of business. He agreed that the Lord had blessed him for his obedience.

A Family Business

A friend who is a pastor told me that a couple in his congregation was having financial trouble in their business. He asked me if I would pray for them. I agreed. I listened to their story for a while and then suggested that we begin to pray. As usual, according to Matthew 18:20, I declared that "two or three of us had gathered together in the name of Jesus Christ." I said, "Now the Lord is not only indwelling us as individuals, He is also manifesting his presence in the midst of us."

Then I just waited for a few moments until I received a word of knowledge. The word was "Uriah." I knew that Uriah was the husband of Bathsheba and that King David had had Uriah put in the front lines of a battle where there was a high likelihood that he would be killed. That is exactly what happened. Essentially David murdered Uriah so that he could take Bathsheba away from him. Wow! What did all this have to do with the couple who was seated in front of me?

I asked the couple to tell me how they had met each other. I did not sense that their answer was complete. I told them that I had received a word from the Lord. When I spoke that word "Uriah," it seemed like I was able to watch the word traveling from my lips to the couple's ears. When the word hit the wife's ears, she immediately dissolved into tears. "Oh, Lord," she cried, "I knew that you were going to make me confess all of these sins." She went on to describe how she had been married previously. At work she fell in love with another man (her current husband) and colluded with that man to extricate her from her marriage to her first husband. Once the first husband was out of the way (divorced, not murdered), the two now in front of me were free to become husband and wife. But it did not stop there. They went on confessing all sorts of other sins that they had committed. In short, they did not have a business problem—they had a sin problem!

By the time they finished confessing and repenting for all of their sins, I declared that they had been forgiven in the name of the Lord Jesus Christ. As I look back on this event, I think to myself, *How much conventional counseling would have been necessary to achieve the same result? One word from the Lord was all that was needed. The Lord knew exactly how to fix this couple's problem.*[2]

CARING FOR GOD'S CREATION

Heeren's stories may seem a bit strange or unusual. Why would God care about businesses?

To answer this question, it is helpful to go back to the beginning of life on Earth. Adam and Eve lived in the Garden and were asked by God to care for it. It was an intimate partnership between the elements of creation, humans and God. Having received the assignment and the necessary resources to do the job, Adam and Eve carried it out. I am sure that every time they saw a broken branch or a stranded animal, they did whatever was necessary to fix it.

Jesus came to seek, save and restore what was lost, including labor.

For Adam and Eve, taking care of the Garden was an act of worship. God walked with them during the cool of the day, very much the way a senior partner reviews the day's transactions with his junior associates (see Gen. 3:8).

Jesus came to seek, save and restore what was lost, including labor, which was originally a spiritual exercise. This is a very important point, because labor is the heartbeat of the marketplace. Today we live in cities, rather than in the Garden, but the assignment remains intact. Whatever is wrong must be fixed as part of our assignment. The earth is God's creation, and we have been asked to care for it (see Gen. 1:28). But how do we do it?

If every believer will go to work fully convinced that he or she is worshiping God through labor and that every constructive action at work is a form of caring for God's creation, our cities will be transformed. Better yet, *we* will be transformed. If every time a janitor sweeps a floor, a clerk enters a transaction, or a broker closes a deal, he or she does it as an expression of worship to God, the kingdom of God will definitely be in evidence all over the city.

In this context it will not be unusual to go into boardrooms or to job sites like Rick Heeren does. Corporations are part of our modern-day garden. In the Garden, seeds and trees yielded fruit to nurture Adam and Eve as well as the animals. Corporations fulfill the same mission today. In the Garden, if the trees died, the source of food died also. Today when corporations fail, the source of income for food disappears. We must care for them the way Adam and Eve cared for the trees and the animals in the Garden.

Whatever needs fixing we should fix, relying on the power and the provision of God. This is what He described when He told Adam and Eve to be fruitful, multiply, rule over everything and have access to the source of provision (see Gen. 1:28-30). This is what He tells us as marketplace Christians today. In the next chapter we are going to see in greater detail how everyone can do it.

Notes
1. Ed Silvoso, *That None Should Perish* (Ventura, CA: Regal Books, 1994), pp. 222-223.
2. Rick Heeren, *Thank God It's Monday: How to Take God to Work With You* (San Jose, CA: Transformational Publications, 2004), n.p. Used by permission.

FOUR STEPS
TO FINDING
YOUR DESTINY
IN THE
MARKETPLACE

In today's global community, the greatest channel of distribution for "salt and light" is the business community . . . the marketplace.

BILL POLLARD, CHAIRMAN, SERVICEMASTER CORPORATION

Martin Luther King, Sr., the father of the civil rights-movement leader, worked at a stable during the day while completing his education at night. It was a tough and grueling job. One day he did not have enough time to clean himself up after work and went to school straight from the stable. When he got to class, someone said with the clear intent to hurt him, "Martin, you smell like a mule." To this he replied, "It is true. But as long as I don't *think* like one, it does not matter."

It does not matter where you find yourself in the marketplace today. What is important is that you embrace your calling to transform that place by using the power that God has made available to you. Joseph's starting point was the slave block in Egypt, but ultimately he ended up running the empire. This is also true of Daniel, who, in addition to being enslaved and deported to a foreign land, was forcibly turned into a eunuch. Nevertheless he became the number one person in the kingdom in charge of all the affairs of state. Norm Miller, Interstate Battery Systems chairman of the board and a marketplace Christian, started out as a traveling salesman. With Miller at the helm, Interstate has become a world-leader in manufacturing batteries. The company's official mission statement reveals the reason behind its success: "To glorify God as we supply our customers worldwide with top quality, value-priced batteries, related electrical power-source products, and distribution services."[1]

Do not let your current circumstances prevent you from seeing God's purpose for your life. If you are overwhelmed, there is someone who understands exactly how you feel: Jesus. In Luke 9, our Lord was so buffeted by discouragement that He was tempted to quit. In a rare moment of utter frustration He demanded, "O unbelieving and perverse generation. . . . How long shall I stay with you and put up with you?" (Luke 9:41, *NIV*). He did not address those strong words to His enemies but to His own disciples, the Twelve. Obviously the Lord was frustrated by the apparent lack of connection between the mission He had and what was going on around Him.

What triggered this unusual outburst was the fact that one demon had defeated His disciples (see Luke 9:39-41). This came on the heels of a succession of attacks orchestrated by Satan—we see Jesus running into demon after demon, culminating with an entire legion. While this was going on, the religious leaders were plotting to kill Jesus, something that His own neighbors also tried to do (see Luke 3—8).

The spiritual climate was so hostile that even John the Baptist saw his own convictions shaken, and Jesus' disciples found themselves working for the devil, albeit unknowingly (see Luke 9:51-56). Even the Father became exasperated and had to rebuke Peter, James and John from a cloud. I doubt that the worse day at the office can come close to a reprimand directly from God. No wonder Jesus felt tempted to throw in the towel. I am sure you can relate to this.

However, everything changed in the next chapter. First, Jesus focused Himself on the harvest: "[It] is plentiful, but the laborers are few" (Luke 10:2). He recruited a new batch of about 70 disciples. He gave them specific instructions, which they followed faithfully. As a result, shortly afterward we read that Jesus rejoiced greatly in the Holy Spirit and began to praise God for the things that were going on around Him (see Luke 10:21).

The reason for Jesus' joy was that His disciples had successfully carried out their assignment and, in the process, defeated every demon they had run into. They declared, "Lord, even the demons are subject to us!" (Luke 10:17), and even Satan had fallen down to Earth (see Luke 10:21). What a change in the spiritual climate!

What was it that triggered it?

To find the answer to this question we need to understand that the fundamental difference between the Twelve and the Seventy is that even though both groups loved Jesus, the Twelve also resented sinners. In fact, they were not at all bashful about it. One time they asked Jesus to dismiss the multitudes who had interrupted a spiritual retreat they were having with Him (see Luke 9:9-13). When the Lord overruled them, they objected to the idea of feeding all of the people who had gathered. Not long after that event Peter tried to permanently move away from sinners by volunteering to build tabernacles for Jesus and His guests on the top of a mountain (see Luke 9:33). At one point, James and John offered to command fire from heaven to burn the lost (see Luke 9:54).

On the other hand, the Seventy were not deterred when Jesus told them, "I send you out as *lambs* in the midst of *wolves*" (Luke 10:3, emphasis added). Lambs do not gravitate naturally toward wolves. To the contrary, they run away from them. Nevertheless Jesus asked them to overrule their natural desires and to seek out wolves. He also gave them very detailed instructions on how to proceed.

First, they were to speak peace to the wolves (see Luke 10:5) and fellowship with them—"eating and drinking what they give you" (Luke 10:7). Next they were to care for their needs—"if anyone is sick, heal them" (Luke 10:9)—and to proclaim that the kingdom of God had come near them.

The Seventy followed Jesus' instructions, and as a result demons became subject to them—even Satan lost his position of power over the region (see Luke 10:17-18). Accounts of very intense demonic activity are recorded in the first nine chapters of Luke, yet practically none appear after chapter 10. Only two demons are mentioned in the next 14 chapters (see Luke 11:14; 13:10-13), and both demons departed without a struggle; they did not even make a noise. What a contrast to the cocky demons who taunted and shouted at Jesus and are found throughout the first nine chapters.[2]

The reason for this extraordinary development is that Jesus used the Seventy to change the spiritual climate over the entire region. This is a principle that is available to us today. Maybe the spiritual atmosphere in your section of the marketplace is as bad, or worse, than what Jesus experienced. Perhaps you are also tempted to quit. Keep the similarities going by emulating what Jesus did in response, as recounted in Luke 10. First, focus on the lost and recognize that there is a plentiful harvest of people who need to be brought in. Second, accept the challenge not to shy away from the harvest field; instead, go deeper into it. Then, once you are in it, follow the same four steps that gave so much victory to the Seventy—blessing, fellowship, care and proclamation.

The marketplace version of these four actions is to join the system, embrace it, improve it and bring the kingdom of God to it.

JOIN THE SYSTEM

If you hold a job, you are already *somewhere* in the marketplace. It does not matter how undesirable your job is or how you got it. What is important is that you be in the system, because God has a purpose for you to fulfill in the marketplace. Consequently, make peace with your job by accepting it as God's starting point for you. Speak peace to it. Thank God for it. Do not let the odorous sin around it prevent you from introducing the sweet aroma of grace. Take a positive posture.

You live in an imperfect world and work in the marketplace that at present is under the control of the evil one. Consequently, you can find plenty of reasons to be upset, even angry, at the marketplace in general and at your job in particular. However, anger gives the devil an opening into a Christian's life. An angry Christian poses no threat to Satan. In fact, it gives him room to work (see Eph. 4:26-27). Anger neutralizes our effectiveness because it is the opposite of grace, and grace is God's remedy to the evil caused by sin.

A Gift from God

Joseph, Daniel and Esther had to make peace and accept situations that were not what they would have chosen, yet they did because they wanted God to be able to reveal His purposes for them. Joseph had to forgive his brothers and overcome the bitterness which, humanly speaking, he was entitled to hold because he had been thrown in a pit and sold into slavery. Daniel had to come to grips with the fact that he was taken away from his homeland and that his manhood was obliterated, forever. Esther had to love a king she did not choose and who had no affection for her people. They all recognized that no matter how much evil had been inflicted upon them, God would eventually use it for good. This was made possible by their conviction that God had a destiny greater and better than their present circumstances. By holding on to that conviction they were able to excel at jobs and assignments that, on the surface, were unappealing, in some cases degrading. If they had quit because their tasks were humiliating, they would never have fulfilled their destinies. This is why it is essential for you take the first step and become part of the marketplace; then accept and sanctify your station in the marketplace.

I suggest that right now you declare that your job is God's gift to you. Your attitude will determine the outcome. Attitude always determines altitude. In marriage, if you think you have married the wrong person but choose to treat him or her like the right one, that person will turn into the right one and you will have a wonderful marriage. But if you married the right person yet treat him or her as the wrong one, that person will turn into the wrong one. The same is true with your job.

You need to be in the system to start the transformation process, and most likely at first the system will be extremely imperfect, but God will not transform it in order to put you in it. On the contrary, He has placed you in it to bring transformation to it. You are the change agent! When you accept this assignment, you will create a monumental problem for the devil because light, no matter how small, will start to invade his kingdom.

Embrace the System

The next step is to embrace your job. It could well be that God may eventually lead you to another job. But until that time comes, you need to give everything you have to your current one. Doing so allows God to move you from victory to victory.

It is not enough to bless and to speak peace to your job. You need to make it a two-way street, very much the way an embrace takes the participation of two people. You must put your arms around it and also let your job embrace you. This is the corporate equivalent of fellowship. In Luke 10 fellowship means that the disciples ate and drank what the wolves put before them. I am sure by the time they were done eating and drinking, their relationship had improved substantially. Make a list of all the good things that your job has to offer, and then affirm them. Make a declaration that you wholeheartedly embrace your job. Joseph did this when he embraced the system of slavery. He could have chosen to remain static but instead he served his masters with extraordinary diligence. The same situation was true of Esther. She served and ministered to her husband and to Haman, not once, but twice. I am sure it must have been difficult for Esther to embrace her job as a queen when she knew that one of the guests was so evil and sought the destruction of her people. But she did not let this distract her from doing the best possible job. She was casting her cares on the Lord, even when she did not know or understand how He was going to come through. Of course, He came through as He always does and delivered Esther's people from the hand of Haman.

So often Christians in the marketplace project tremendous rejection toward the workplace. They point to the flaws in the system and thus condemn it. We should not do this. When the adulterous woman stood before Jesus, He did not focus on the sins that had ruined her but on the hope that lay ahead: "Go your way. From now on sin no more" (John 8:11). When light and darkness meet, guess who wins? Greater is the One who is in us than the one who is in the world.

Dave Wendorff is a developer who builds homes. Sometimes he and his partner build entire neighborhoods. My wife and I have known Dave and his wife, Kristen, for many years. One day Dave and I were talking about the steps a Christian can take in the marketplace, and he asked how this would play out in his job. It soon became clear to Dave that every building project provides him with the unique opportunity to be a pastor to hundreds of people who work for him—carpenters, plumbers, electricians, architects, engineers and real estate agents, even city officials with whom he has to interface. He decided that from that point on every time he and his partner buy a parcel of land and hire contractors and subcontractors, he will consider them part of his congregation of "lost sheep." He will speak peace over them when they submit their bids. He will fellowship with them while they work for him. He will pray for God's miracles to benefit them as he becomes aware of their needs, and eventually when miracles touch them, he will let them know that the kingdom of God had come near.

Furthermore, Dave will prayer drive and prayer walk the developments, blessing first the vacant lots and then the houses as they go up, praying for the safety of the workers and praying for God to bring the right people to live in them. He will also pray for Christians with the gift of evangelism to move into the neighborhood. All of a sudden what to

Dave used to be a secular job has become a ministry simply because he decided to apply the business version of the four steps outlined by Jesus in Luke 10.

Improve the System

The next step is to improve the system. In the same fashion that the Seventy were told to heal the sick in the homes of those with whom they had fellowship, you and I are instructed by the Lord to make things better at work, especially those things that are not doing so well. When you make peace with your job, you neutralize the evil elements that have created strife between you and your work. When you embrace it, you make it a part of your life that makes God's blessings extend to your job.

God bestowed blessings upon Egypt, Babylon and Persia on account of Joseph, Daniel and Esther. They were able to improve the system and, in so doing, they proved to their kings that God cared for their nations. What could be dearer to a king than his kingdom? Likewise, when you improve systems at work, you convey a deeply appreciated message to your boss, partner, associates or employees. Furthermore, when the improvement is the result of divine intervention—such as what happened to Rick Heeren—you point them toward God. When this happens, people *always* want to know more about such a God.

In July 2000 Harvest Evangelism facilitated a two-week-long prayer evangelism thrust in Buenos Aires, Argentina. About 200 overseas trainees were a part of this summer short-term missions project. We used the same hotel that we had also booked for our international conference the following October. We heard that the hotel was struggling financially, so we prayed for God's hand to bless the management. On a Wednesday the manager asked our accountant and me if we would be willing to advance him some funds that would apply to the conference we would be holding in October. I did not have the money, so I told him, "Neither silver nor gold have I but what I have I give to you," paraphrasing Peter and John (see Acts 3:5-6).

Puzzled by my response, he asked me what I meant. I said that we would pray that God would give him a financial miracle. He told me that if God was going to do something, He had better do it quickly and make it big, because he needed a lot of money *pronto*. I assured him that our accountant and I would pray right away and that we were certain that God would listen to our prayers. At that moment he confessed that he did not believe much in prayer. I reassured him by stating that it did not matter, since we were the ones who would pray and we did believe in prayer. A little bit more encouraged now, he confided that he was not sure he believed in Jesus. Again I reassured him by stating that after we had prayed he would certainly want to believe in Jesus.

We asked that God would perform a financial miracle for the hotel. It was 6:00 P.M. when we prayed, after which we left his office. At 6:30 P.M. the manager received a call from the international airport. A 747 airplane had been unable to take off, the flight had been delayed, and lodging was needed for about 200 passengers—they would pay in cash. That was a quick answer, but there was more to come. Over the next two days the hotel received enough reservations to fill all of its rooms for the next 70 days!

On Friday morning the manager asked to see us again. When we went to his office, he looked different. I was no longer "Mr. Silvoso" but "Pastor Silvoso." He went on to tell us everything that had happened since our prayer on Wednesday. Then he asked, "What does this mean?" Before we knew it, we found ourselves leading him to the Lord. Later on he came to the room where our team was having breakfast and gave public testimony of his salvation. When we returned in October, he introduced us to the owner who was eager to learn more about "this God who blesses businesses." Less than an hour into the conversation the owner also received the Lord. Five days later he asked us to speak to his 12 managers. When we did, all of them received the Lord. Nothing points marketplace people toward the Lord better than when they see a miracle *in the marketplace*!

Bringing the Kingdom to Your Job

Finally, declare that the kingdom of God has come to the place where you work. This is not an abstract declaration. You are the light of the world; therefore, you are able to bless your job, embrace it and bring to bear the power of God on the areas that require miracles. These three steps determine the advent of the kingdom of God. Once the kingdom of God is in place, it is bound to expand. It is very important to understand that the kingdom of God is always *expansive*, never *regressive*. If you fail to grasp this, you may find yourself neutralized in your endeavors to see the marketplace transformed.

The following story eloquently illustrates what it means to see the kingdom of God break through in the workplace. It is the story of a high-ranking executive in a large European telecommunications corporation.

Even though the executive had been a believer since childhood, he was very skeptical about the supernatural dimension of the kingdom of God. He had his doubts until he had a powerful encounter with the Lord that brought renewal to *all* aspects of his life, including his business career.

> You are the light of the world; therefore, you are able to bless your job.

The day he learned he was to be a shepherd to the employees in his department, he quickly took action. The next day he went to work before anyone else was there and blessed the working space of each single employee in his department. He did this day after day and, soon enough, a significant improvement in the spiritual climate happened. This became evident when sick leaves and conflict levels in his department became dramatically lower than in the rest of the company. The CEO asked the Christian executive if he had an explanation. "It's God!" he said, and he went on to explain how he had put a canopy of prayer over the department. At that precise moment he obtained great favor with his boss.

When it was decided to construct a new corporate headquarters, the Christian executive was put in charge of the project. From the time they started to dig until the facilities were finished he made sure that prayer covered everything. The official department in charge of keeping records on accidents on the project approached him perplexed by the lack of accidents in the building process. They scrutinized the records to see if there was underreporting or if someone had tampered with the books. They found that everything was in complete order, but they still could not understand why the level of accidents was so much lower than expected. "It is God," the Christian executive said, and he went on to give them the same speech he had given his boss.

As the man in charge of the building project, he was asked to give a speech at the dedication. He used that opportunity to give God all the glory and to bless those in attendance.

But these two events were just the beginning. Key people in the corporation, the Christian executive included, were working on a book on environmental preservation at the time the company had submitted a bid for a major international communication contract. The time was fast approaching for the bid to be awarded, and there was some concern that it would go to someone else. The CEO, who was not a Christian, approached the Christian executive with a request: "Will you ask this God of yours what it is that we must do to win this bid?" The Christian executive did so, listened for a word from God and when he received it, he reported back to his boss: "I am not sure whether this is from the Lord, but this is what I would do." He suggested they use the book on the environment. The CEO took the advice, went to the meeting and presented the information on the environment, even though it had *nothing* to do with what the bid was about. This was followed by two weeks of absolute silence from the buyers while they considered the bids. It was a time of testing for this Christian executive. Had he done the right thing? Did he hear from God? Finally the word came that they got the deal mainly because they were the only bidder who had an environmental plan. They later sold the deal and made a profit of approximately $1 billion (U.S.). Needless to say, the Christian executive's favor increased dramatically in the eyes of the top management.

About a year ago this executive gave a lecture on future solutions for energy scarcity to more than 100 industry professionals at an international forum. Toward the end of the lecture, quoting from Genesis, he spoke about the need for humans to be responsible stewards on God's behalf and take care of nature. Framing such appeal with biblical principles is not politically correct. Predictably, there were mixed reactions, some even hostile. Later on, as the delegates gathered in the bar, there was more discussion on the subject. It was so intense that everybody agreed he should speak further on it *right away*!

The group marched back into the auditorium where this market-place Christian spoke about God the creator, our stewardship on Earth, Jesus and salvation. Unbelievably, this resulted in requests for prayer from the audience. As he started to pray and bless those interested, more and more delegates came forward until he ended up laying hands on every person in the room. This was not a revival meeting but a convention of more than 100 high-ranking energy executives from several nations. There is a biblical precedent for this. It is found in Luke 16:16: "The gospel of the kingdom of God is preached, and everyone is forcing his way into it."

As I was working on this section of my book, I tried to call this Christian businessman. I could not reach him because he was at a celebration banquet. So, through a mutual friend, I relayed my questions to him. However, what the banquet was all about is *extremely* exciting. Key executives were celebrating the tangible evidence of the kingdom of God in his company's balance sheet. In 1996 the department this Christian executive heads up was $13 million (U.S.) in the red, but in 2001 it produced a surplus of $1.3 million (U.S.)! "There is no way this could happen without the intervention of the Lord," he said.

It is very important to remember that this ocean of blessings began at the headwaters of a very tiny creek. The key, the origin, was simple obedience. It started on the day this marketplace Christian decided to make blessing his corporation part of his job description.

Yes, it is possible to bring the kingdom of God to your job!

FIVE LEVELS OF MISERY AND COMFORT

In a POW camp there are five levels on the misery-comfort axis. At the lowest level are those people who believe that the war will never be won and consequently they have resigned themselves to die with dignity. They live the best possible lives while looking forward to an honorable death.

The next level consists of those who believe that even though the war is lost, they can do something to improve their conditions inside the barracks in the POW camp. To that effect they organize themselves and provide comfort and assistance to each other, especially to those who are distressed the most.

The middle level encompasses those who believe that even though the war will not be won, they have a right to negotiate with the commandant to improve camp conditions. They are not satisfied with just mending their barracks; their goal is to improve the camp also. As a result of their determination and organization they are able to secure longer exercise times and larger quantities of bread and water, all in accordance with the Geneva Convention statutes regarding POWs. They do not always get everything they want, but sometimes they do. When this happens, they consider it a major victory.

The next level up consists of those who believe that they can and should take over the camp. To that effect they organize and train themselves, secure weapons and eventually liberate their fellow prisoners. As soon as they are in control, they kick the commandant and his soldiers out and fortify the camp to prevent them from coming back. Living conditions improve dramatically as the ex-POWs now thrive in their newfound freedom. They hope their commander in chief will win the war before they die, and to that effect they look forward to the day they will be set free. In the meantime, they enjoy their much-improved camp, especially the fact that the evil oppressors have been deposed, even though they lurk menacingly nearby on the outside.

The fifth and last level represents those who are convinced that they can take over the camp and do everything that those on level four did, but they also believe that they should train the newly liberated soldiers and send them out to free prisoners in other camps. Their ultimate objective is to liberate every POW in every camp.

Misery and Comfort Levels in the Marketplace

These five levels of misery and comfort are present in the Church today, particularly in marketplace Christians.

Christians at the lowest level have no hope that anything will change for the better, but they are determined to live the best possible life in the midst of a pitiful situation. Their determination is admirable, but they are of little use as far as pushing back the kingdom of darkness.

Next are those who believe that some basic elements in the marketplace can be changed and, therefore, they launch and run programs. They have no hope for a takeover of the camp, but they are determined to make the best out of a bad situation.

Then come those people who believe that a certain level of revival in the marketplace is possible. They enjoy it occasionally, but when it happens, it is only the equivalent of increased rations and extended recreation time within the barbed-wire-fenced camps. Those few good times remind them of the day when the Lord will come to rescue them.

Then there are those who take over and establish the kingdom of God where the devil's kingdom used to be. However, these people do not dare to go beyond that. Rather than moving forward, they put the wagons in a circle and fortify their positions in order to establish an outpost of heaven on Earth.

Finally, we find those who believe that the enemy's camp can and should be overrun, his goods looted and the former captives trained to go out and bring liberation to people in other camps until the last one has been set free. This group represents the new paradigm that this book is about.

The jeepney driver I wrote about in chapter 8 is a classic example of this paradigm at work. Not satisfied with turning a bar into a church, he and his associates reached out to other businesses and established the kingdom of God in 14 of them. This group is determined not to stop until the entire marketplace in their city has been transformed. Will they succeed? I do not know, but it is always better to shoot for a star, even if we miss, than to aim for a skunk and hit it!

Taking the First Step

The key remains the fourfold approach coming out of Luke 10: bless, fellowship, care and proclaim. In the marketplace, as noted above, this means being in the system, embracing it and improving it so that the kingdom of God can come to it. Let me encourage you to get going. Do not let anything stop you. A journey of a thousand miles begins with the first step.

If you work for an ungodly boss or a corporation where the spiritual climate is repressive, do not let that prevent you from moving forward. I doubt that your boss or any of your associates can be worse that Daniel's, Joseph's or Esther's bosses. They served evil, pagan, idol-worshiping kings but that did not deter them from fulfilling their destinies. You may say that your job is less than desirable. Well, after Daniel interpreted the dream, what job did he receive? The king appointed him to head the witches and warlocks union of Babylon. What did Daniel do? Did he decline? No, he took the job and brought the kingdom of God to the place where Satan was. Light always defeats darkness.

Richard Gazowsky, who serves as a pastor in San Francisco, was going through a discouraging time. Overwhelmed by the difficulties buffeting him, his family and his congregation, he began to walk on the shoreline late into the night. In a very gloomy mood he cried out to God for help while pointing out to Him the spiritual darkness that had enveloped everything in his life and ministry. All of a sudden the Lord directed him to look toward the ocean. When he did, the Lord asked, "What do you see?" Richard replied, "Darkness. That is all there is." The Lord instructed him to look again. Richard replied a second time that all he saw was darkness except for three tiny lights in the distance. The Lord asked him, "What do you see besides darkness?" He answered, "Three tiny lights. That is all." To this the Lord said, "Do not miss the point that there are more lights than darkness. Darkness is *always* singular whereas light can be plural, and in this case it is."

What an incredible truth: Light can always increase, but darkness can only decrease. Take heart and begin to implement these four steps to bring transformation to the marketplace. The key is to move forward. Jesus said that the gates of hell shall not prevail against the Church (see Matt. 16:18). Gates are defensive weapons, not offensive ones. This means that the only way they can prevail is if you do not attack them. But if you do, they will not prevail. Move forward!

Notes

1. "Mission Statement," *Interstatebatteries.com.* http://www.interstatebatteries.com/ www_2001/content/about_us/mission.asp (accessed February 6, 2002).
2. For a detailed explanation of how to change the spiritual climate of a city, see my book *Prayer Evangelism* (Ventura, CA: Regal Books, 2000).

YOUR DESTINY: SAVING THE NATION

God has strategically placed His children in key leadership roles in the
midst of our nation and our world just for such a time as this.

HENRY BLACKABY, BAPTIST PRESS

Gideon was busy trying to save himself. The angel of the Lord sent him to save the nation instead. Gideon had no strength, but the angel said, "Go" (see Judg. 6:14). Obedience rates higher with God than our attempts at understanding the command He is giving us. The following is the story of a young marketplace lady whom God used to bring hope to millions in the aftermath of the greatest terrorist attack in America. On that day, she surely felt she had no strength, yet she obeyed God's leading and went.

September 11, 2001, is a date we will never forget. The image of the World Trade Center hit by the first plane was shocking enough, but when a second plane crashed into the other tower, in plain view of millions, the shock reached a level none of us had ever experienced. As we watched what was before us in disbelief, our dread reached even greater depths as both buildings collapsed. In a matter of seconds two of the tallest buildings in the world, the international center of commerce, became a burning pile of rubble.

Our consternation turned to panic and abhorrence when we learned that a third plane had hit the Pentagon—until then America's impregnable fortress—and that this was the work of terrorists. Glued to our television sets, we lost our innocence. Then a fourth plane went down in a field in Pennsylvania. America was being violated in plain view, and some people on the other side of the world were rejoicing while we wept.

The next few days were a time of bottomless anguish, deep confusion and never-ending consternation as the nation struggled to find its bearings. Many of us woke up in the morning hoping that it all had been a nightmare, but the morning news told us otherwise. With grim faces and somber voices framed by horrific pictures, the anchorpersons reminded us that we did not imagine it, that indeed thousands of people had died and that the nation, once thought inviolable, had been violently wounded.

However, something happened on Friday of that somber week that caused the emotional roller-coaster to stop. A prayer service at the National Cathedral in Washington, D.C., attended by the president and countless functionaries and dignitaries, was broadcast to the nation and to the world. All major faiths were represented in the program, but the service was distinctly Christian. Billy Graham preached his best sermon ever and pulled no punches when it came to presenting the gospel in a clear and compelling manner. The president also took to the podium and ministered faith and hope to millions of people who were struggling with despair. As people watched the service unfold, the most extraordinary impartation of faith and hope took place. Millions were reassured that God was on the throne and that His hand still protects those who seek refuge in Him. Viewers could feel the spiritual climate improving with every minute of the program.

> Never has the Christian faith shone so brightly in the midst of so much darkness and touched such a vast audience.

This service became the most-watched religious service in the history of the world. In nation after nation, through simultaneous translation where necessary, the majority of the population of the world heard the Word of God. Never has the Christian faith shone so brightly in the midst of so much darkness and touched such a vast audience. From that moment on, hope retook the upper hand and prayer became the vehicle of a God who cared. The service on Friday, September 14, 2001, turned the spiritual tide. Even though more trials would come, the moorings of Christianity were in plain view for all to see that evil will not overtake good.

GOD CHOSE CHARITY

What very few people know is the role that a young marketplace lady played in putting that service together. Charity Wallace is her name. She is 26 years old and she works at the White House as part of the president's advance team. When the moment came to entrust someone with a key role in organizing a national prayer service to minister to the nation and to the world, God chose Charity.

However, it could have gone quite a different way. Charity and her workmates at the White House experienced the attack firsthand. In the midst of the ensuing confusion there was a moment when she was tempted to get in her car and drive cross-country to California, to the safety of her home and the comforting embrace of her parents. But she did not. This is how she recalls it:

Tuesday, September 11, 2001, began as an ordinary day for me—as
I am sure it did for most of us. After arriving at work at 8:00 A.M.,
I got to my desk and put my headphones on to listen to Pastor
Jack Hayford on the radio from 8:00 A.M. to 8:30 A.M., just as I
always do. Then a coworker, Stephanie, and I went across the
street to get bagels.

We were returning when I saw in one of the offices a TV set
showing scenes of the World Trade Towers on fire. I asked why
the World Trade Center was on fire, and a slightly panicked
intern informed us that two planes had crashed into the WTC.
It did not register yet—but the possibility of terrorism started to
set in.

I just wanted to get to our office, so we could watch the
news. As Steph and I rounded the corner, another colleague
came out of her office with her eyes wide with fear. She was trying to describe what was going on. I realized things were terribly
wrong. I began thinking and suggesting to those in my office
that we should leave.

I did not leave immediately but began praying for the Lord's
protection. A few moments later, CNN began reporting that the
White House was being evacuated. The scene in the halls of the
Old Executive Office Building (OEOB) was surreal. People were
sprinting out of the building—fleeing to the nearest exits in a
mass exodus. Hearts racing, we also began running down the
stairs, contemplating which way to go. It was like watching a
movie, yet being a part of it as well. I saw the vice president's
motorcade staging outside the West Wing and U.S. Secret Service
getting set for a departure. The gates on West Executive Drive
were open to aid our quick escape, and uniformed officers were
yelling, "Run!"

I left a message on my parents' message machine that I was
evacuating the White House and to please pray! As we were
rounding the corner toward Seventeenth Street—everyone's focus
turned toward the sky. A passenger plane was flying above the
White House. It was making erratic turns.

People were screaming to uniformed officers and Secret Service agents, "Where are we supposed to go?!" Their response was simply "Run as fast as you can—get as far AWAY from the White House as possible." What a scene this frantic and mass exodus must have been for those people stopped in their cars on Seventeenth Street.

I ended up speaking with my mother [on a cell phone] while running to my car. I was trying to devise an escape plan, as we were uncertain if the terror was over. Stephanie and I jumped into my car near the Washington Monument—which was scary, because we thought they might try to fly a plane into the monument too—and headed onto Constitution Avenue. I prayed that the Lord would surround my car with His angels to protect us on our way home—claiming God's promise in Psalm 91:7 that "a thousand would fall at my side and ten thousand at my right hand, but it would not come near me."

Smoke was now rising from the Pentagon. The plane that had once hovered overhead had disappeared. We were heading toward my house but were unsure of each move. I knew that driving by the State Department was a risk, but the quickest route home was over the Roosevelt Bridge. I was nervous about getting onto a bridge, but that was the only way to get out of the District and get home. Safely crossing the bridge, we got onto the highway to take us home. At that point, radio reports announced that the first tower had collapsed. It was so surreal and very frightening. Also, now I could not reach anyone on the phone—lines were down.

My first instinct was to drive across the country to be with my family. I began packing a suitcase at this point and started plotting my journey home. As I did this, a small voice inside of me let me know that I was to stay put—*this* is when faith is tested—where the rubber meets the road. This was confirmed by my mother's conversation with Pastor Scott Bauer, the senior pastor at my church in Los Angeles. Scott said that the Lord gave him a word for me—he said, "The Lord has put Charity at the White House for THIS moment. She is there not only to do the president's schedule but also to be there for this moment—to intercede for the president and the nation at this time. Just as in the time of Esther, 'for such a time as this.'"

This is a tall charge for a girl who wants to be with her family and friends in California. I then received a call on Tuesday night instructing me to be in the office on Wednesday morning. It was difficult to return, but there were things to be done. A bit shaken but with supernatural peace in my heart, I went to work Wednesday morning. About 11:00 A.M. I was asked to gather up all the information from the National Cathedral Prayer Service I had organized for the inauguration. We learned at 5:00 P.M. on Wednesday afternoon that the president and Mrs. Bush would be going to the National Cathedral for a National Day of Prayer and Remembrance on Friday [September 14] at 12 noon.

We had had 31 days to plan the inaugural; now we had only 31 hours to plan the National Day of Prayer and Remembrance for the nation. It is amazing to see how the Lord is so faithful, even in this. It was such an honor to have been the lead (planner) for the prayer service during the inauguration, but He knew that I would need to have all this information for *this* day.

We worked round the clock planning the program, inviting speakers, arranging plane transportation with the Department of Transportation and FAA [all airports were closed immediately after the attack]. On Thursday, in the midst of meetings and planning sessions, we were evacuated again. It is scary to come out of an office and see people running down the stairs trying to get to safety. But deep down I knew God was with us! God truly had His hand on this event, as it came together so smoothly and beautifully.

On the following Sunday, I was reflecting on how life has changed so dramatically, how life might never be the same. God reminded me, "Yes, life has changed, but I (God) am the SAME." He is the same yesterday, today and forever! That verse means so much more to me now.[1]

Charity did not hide the fact that right after the attack she was tempted to get as far from Washington, D.C., as she possibly could. But she chose to stay, even though her natural strength was limited. As a result, God used her to play a key role in putting together a service that ministered to millions around the world. She is not a professional preacher, but God used her to preach the Word to millions through that national prayer service. Recognizing that God had placed her in the White House for a strategic time and making herself available to God were the keys. Choosing obedience over fear made the difference. Instead of a girl trying to save herself, she became a minister by proxy to millions.

Charity's story is similar to Gideon's. When we think of Gideon, we usually associate him with heroism, but he was not always a superman. When the angel of the Lord spoke to him, he was busy hiding some wheat in the winepress before fleeing to the mountains. It had been 40 years since God had moved in the land of Israel. He had last moved when He used Deborah to destroy the Syrian army. In the ensuing years the Midianites had grown strong and had brutally oppressed Israel. Every year, during harvesttime, the Midianites would invade Israel and, while the people of God fled to hide in caves, their enemies ate their crops and stole their animals. The Israelites were so demoralized that they came to accept as inevitable that the enemy would dispossess them and force them to live off of leftovers. They had lost hope.

> Obedience in spite of fear is what made Gideon such a hero.

GOD CHOSE GIDEON

Gideon was no different from Charity—he had tried to save some wheat for himself. But the angel of the Lord spoke to him, "The LORD is with you, O valiant warrior" (Judg. 6:12).

Gideon was neither valiant nor a warrior. He was gathering grain and preparing to flee. Nevertheless the angel of God called him a mighty warrior. Why? Because God always has a higher opinion of us than the one we have of ourselves. He is able to see us, not through the grim grid of past failures, but through the pristine prism of future victories He has in store for us.

Gideon questioned the angel's affirming statement by pointing out that it was inconsistent with the reality around him. "If the Lord is with us, why then has all this happened to us? And where are His miracles which our fathers told us about?" His conclusion was disheartening, "The LORD has abandoned us and given us into the hands of Midian" (Judg. 6:13).

The Lord did not answer any of Gideon's questions. Instead God gave him a command: "Go in this your strength and deliver the [nation]" (Judg. 6:14). How much strength did Gideon have? Practically none, but God was not interested in his strength; rather, He was concerned about his obedience. Even though Gideon was full of doubts, he did everything the Lord asked him to do. He tore down the altars in his father's house. He did it at night for fear of his neighbors—but he did it. He put a fleece before God, asking for a sign; and when he got the sign, he asked for confirmation because he was still buffeted by doubts. When the Lord told him to go to the enemy's camp and to take his servant with him if he was afraid, he took his servant. So we can see that he was afraid; nonetheless, he went. Obedience in spite of fear is what made Gideon such a hero. He was not by nature a brave man, but he was obedient by choice, and as a result a nation was delivered.

HAS GOD CHOSEN YOU?

The heart of the city is the marketplace. To change a city, the marketplace must be transformed. This is your call. This is your destiny. Focus on God's purpose for you and not on any of the fears that may be lurking around or inside of you. Obedience rates higher than knowledge.

The first humans, Adam and Eve, lived in the Garden. God told them to take care of it and to rule over everything. He also told them that He had provided for all their needs (see Gen. 1:28). Today we no longer live in the Garden but in cities. Cities are dear to God. We have only two accounts of Jesus weeping: once for His beloved friend Lazarus and once for Jerusalem—a city. Cities are the modern equivalent of the

Garden. God's command is to take care of them. If all marketplace Christians can understand this, they will go to work every day knowing that their job is their ministry. Every time they enter a transaction, build a wall or return a phone call, they will see themselves as taking care of God's creation. Work will be worship, as it was in the Garden, and God will come down *in the cool of the day* to discuss the day's events with them.

As part of taking care of God's creation, marketplace Christians will exercise spiritual authority over all power of the evil one (see Luke 10:17-21). As we do this, the kingdom of darkness will recede, and God's kingdom will be established so that His will shall be done on Earth *as it is done in heaven.*

This is not a fantasy; rather, it is the assignment that God has given to us. In order to be able to embrace this assignment and carry it out we need to deal with a major inconsistency in our theology. We have no problem believing that Satan was able to defile the *entire* creation by introducing sin into the lives of Adam and Eve. This is sound doctrine and every Christian will agree with it. However, we do not accept the idea that the grace introduced into our lives by Jesus can redeem the same creation that the original sin defiled. If sin were able to do so much damage, grace would definitely be capable of doing much more restoration, because where sin abounds, grace always overflows.

As Christians we believe that this world will pass away and that we are awaiting new heavens and a new Earth. Few people will argue with this theology. But the fact that the new things are coming should not prevent us from bringing the kingdom of God to this Earth. Our bodies provide a good example. Before coming to Christ they were temples of the devil as we followed the prince of the power of the air (see Eph. 2:1-3). But when Christ came into our lives, our bodies became the temple of the Holy Spirit. Even though we know that our present bodies show the effects of aging and that someday each of us will die, we still take the best possible care of them. The fact that perfect bodies are awaiting us in eternity does not deter us from making our present bodies as godly and healthy as possible. The same logic should be applied to Earth. Until the new one comes, let us bring the kingdom of God to every place on it so that the will of God will be done on Earth as it is done in heaven.

This is why each of us needs to see ourselves as conduits for that grace to redeem the marketplace. It already redeemed you. Now you must become the vehicle to change things around you. This is the will of God and He has already announced it in the heavenly places.

When Gideon and his servant arrived at the enemy's camp, they heard enemy soldiers talk about a dream where a mighty deed brought down the camp of the Midianites. The person who had been given the dream asked for an explanation and was unequivocally told that the interpretation was that they had been delivered into the hands of Gideon and his sword. Gideon was not holding a sword at the moment, nor was he ready to strike. But God had already convinced his enemies that the victory had been awarded to him. God not only had a higher opinion of Gideon than he had of himself, but God also spoke better of him than Gideon spoke of himself.

This same dynamic is true for you today. God looks at you and declares that you are a mighty warrior. He says, "Believe Me when I say that you are such. In whatever strength you have *go* and save the nation instead of trying to save yourself. Stop centering all of your efforts on making your business prosper and begin to work to transform the marketplace. It is not your strength that I am after; it is your obedience."

This is the dilemma that Charity Wallace had to confront. She had to choose between her fears—shouting at her to get in her car and flee to California—and the voice of God—first in her own heart and then confirmed through her pastor, that she was to go back to find her destiny at the White House.

Obedience is what God expects. Lift up your eyes from your immediate needs and fix them on God's eternal destiny for you. He is ready to use you to transform the marketplace. Are you ready?

Note

1. Charity Wallace, "Memoir from the White House" (manuscript, 2001), n.p. Used by permission.

WHY GOD WANTS YOU TO DECLARE CHAPTER 11 BANKRUPTCY

We must begin with God. We are right when, and only when,
we stand in a righteous position relative to God, and we are wrong so
far and so long as we stand in any other position.

A. W. TOZER

In the United States the term "Chapter 11" is often associated with bankruptcy. When it seemed that this was going to be the last chapter of this book, I debated with myself whether I should call it Chapter 11 or not, since that name conjures negative images for people in the marketplace. For a while I referred to it as the epilogue.

However, a closer look at Chapter 11 yields a positive picture, because it is a legal process designed to protect faltering corporations. Basically it creates a legal harbor to serve as protection against secured creditors who could put the corporation out of business through the forced sale of assets.

Under Chapter 11, the corporation must submit to the bankruptcy court a reorganization scheme showing how it plans to get out of its troubles. It must also disclose every detail of its business to the court. Ideally, the plan has to be approved by the creditors, but the judge has the authority to do so unilaterally. The good news is that while in Chapter 11 the corporation is allowed to continue in business.

A more severe bankruptcy scenario is the one known as Chapter 7 (sorry, I could not avoid having a chapter 7 in this book). If the court finds that the corporation is beyond recovery, it orders it into Chapter 7 and all its assets are sold to pay as much of its obligations as possible. Even though many corporations come out of Chapter 11 stronger, no business ever survives Chapter 7.

In the business world, bankruptcy is always triggered by the inability of a corporation to meet financial obligations. In the spiritual world, bankruptcy is the inability to meet God's standards. As you reach the last chapters of this book, you may feel that you need to file for *spiritual* Chapter 11.

In the marketplace, when a corporation declares Chapter 11, in preparation for reorganization, the board of directors must analyze past performance, be willing to correct mistakes and be prepared to realign resources. However, if the judge suspects deceit or incompetence, or if there is a deadlock among the board members, he will appoint a receiver to take over the corporation. It is always to the corporation's advantage to be transparent and forthcoming.

The same is true in the spiritual realm. If done properly, filing for *spiritual* Chapter 11 would make you stronger, not weaker—especially when you consider that the judge, God, will review your case in the context of very favorable jurisprudence (the Bible), your lead attorney is His Son, Jesus, and His associate counsel is the Holy Spirit. Therefore, it is essential that you be transparent and examine yourself in the areas of deceit, incompetence or a deadlock. Otherwise you may be turned over to a spiritual receiver when the spiritual prosecutor (Satan) exposes you. While the judge is still ultimately in control, the appointment of a receiver takes freedom away from the corporation. The same scenario happens in the spirit realm. How this works is shown in the parable of the two debtors. The king threw the second slave in prison (loss of freedom) "until he should pay what was owed" (Matt. 18:30). This is not an exact parallel, of course, but it vividly gets across the point that failing to be transparent with God and with each other causes us to lose control and to be disciplined.

Our Lord spoke words that readily apply to such situations: "Make friends quickly with your opponent at law while you are with him on the way, in order that your opponent may not deliver you to the judge, and the judge to the officer, and you be thrown into prison" (Matt. 5:25). The picture painted by Jesus is of a person who has no case but insists on going to court. The end result is that this person loses control when he or she is thrown into prison. This is what a receiver does—he takes away the freedom of action of those filing for Chapter 11, because their character has been impeached and, as a result, they cannot be trusted to come up with a credible reorganization plan.

THE PROBLEM WITH DECEIT

The most lethal form of deceit is the one brought about by personal sin. Sin is like a powerful drug. After the initial jolt you become progressively addicted until you lose the ability to break free. This in turn leads to dangerous rationalizations. You tell yourself that sin is inevitable and that it will not hurt you. Nothing can be further from the truth! The wages of sin is death (see Rom. 3:23).

You would never work for a person if you knew that instead of giving you a paycheck he would shoot you dead. That is what sin does. It is serious, dangerous and lethal. If there is sin in your life, repent, renounce it and return to the Lord right away. God will not bless you until you have dealt with it because God is holy. In fact, there is no surer way to give the accuser of the brethren (Satan) an opportunity to make a motion requesting the appointment of a spiritual receiver than to try to hide sin (see Rev. 12:10). God will grant Satan's request because He knows that once we reach this level of deceit, we will not be willing to renounce our own sins. This, in turn, calls for a firm hand. In fact, this is what Paul did in Corinth to a person who insisted on justifying sin (see 1 Cor. 5:1-5) and later on to two other individuals (see 1 Tim. 1:20). Because sin is so destructive, God will use whatever means necessary, including Satan, to bring us to a point of repentance.

> **The most lethal form of deceit is brought about by personal sin.**

If a corporation is in trouble because of deceit and it is able to hide the truth from the court, the reorganization plan will not succeed. Deceit is like a cancer. The sooner it is exposed, the better the chances of survival. If there is sin in your life, God wants you to deal with it. He will do anything to get you to that point. Your current spiritual bankruptcy may be His way of dealing with you. He will not permit you to hide your sin any longer, because He knows that sin will ultimately destroy you.

Sin is *never* acceptable. Daniel and Joseph understood this. Joseph went to jail rather than succumb to sexual immorality. Daniel and his companions turned down the king's food on one occasion and faced the fiery furnace on another rather than compromise their convictions. How much God can entrust in you is determined by how much sin you refuse to take from the devil and the flesh. The reverse of this is also true: Yielding to sin drives you away from God, His love and His provision. The farther you get from God, the closer you get to the devil.

Corporate Sin

Sin committed in the context of business is as bad as personal sin. Corporate sins may take the form of broken relationships, contracts and agreements among coworkers or outsiders. Quite often in the competitive atmosphere of the marketplace the fine line that separates persuasion from manipulation, or due diligence from abuse, is overlooked or ignored and people are injured. Marketplace Christians must also deal with this.

A businessman who owns a large company was convicted by the Holy Spirit of taking advantage of a competitor by using unethical practices to win a bid. This happened many years ago, but instead of rationalizing it he called the competitor, apologized to him and sent him a check for the profit he had made on the deal.

This had an immediate positive impact. The competitor, who at the time was a backsliding Christian, came back to the Lord. Since then both men have worked together on business deals that have benefited both of their corporations.

James makes a very important point about unpaid wages, another corporate sin (see Jas. 5:1-8). He writes that those wages testify against the debtor. If such is the case, you are staring at the source of your current troubles. Stealing at work—from a competitor, a partner, an employer or an employee—is as bad as stealing from the offering plate, because your job is your ministry. Make restitution and begin to walk in the spiritual freedom that will come about as a result of it.

Other forms of deceit are more subtle but just as damaging: to believe that secular work is less spiritual than religious work, that God's power and presence cannot manifest themselves in the marketplace as they do in church meetings or that to be able to hear God's voice and instructions we need to withdraw from the marketplace.

Every instance recorded in the Bible where someone met with God, he or she always came out of His presence with specific instructions about something that God wanted done *on Earth*. In fact, with the exception of Paul, who was transported to the third heaven to receive revelations (see 2 Cor. 12:1-4), God was always the One doing the traveling. He must like it down here; otherwise why would He come so often? The idea of removing ourselves from daily routines in order to be spiritual has no biblical basis. Spirituality in the Scriptures is when we implement God's will on Earth, rather than try to subtract ourselves from it and its problems.

Many marketplace Christians face spiritual bankruptcy today because they do not believe that they can hear God's voice at work. They need to expose, renounce and remove such deceit. Then they *can* and *will* hear God's voice in the marketplace! Be encouraged by the fact that every revival listed in the Old Testament was a marketplace-centered revival. The Temple and the altar may have played key roles, but revival always touched people in the marketplace.

SUPERNATURAL EFFICIENCY

Inefficiency is the next factor. This can be defined as "not producing the desired effect, incompetent—lacking sufficient knowledge, skill or ability."[1]

Business can be done God's way or man's way. It is obvious which way will be the most efficient. Many Christians in the marketplace fail because they rely upon carnal instead of spiritual tools (see 2 Cor. 10:3-5). By "carnal" I do not necessarily mean evil tools but simply human wisdom. Of course, God wants Christians to be smart businesspeople and come up with standards such as Ken Blanchard's time-management tools. But we should not be relying upon these as our primary or ultimate guide. If your job is your ministry, then God, who appointed you as a minister, has a supernatural empowerment for you to be able to do it His way.

As I have previously noted, in Exodus 31 we read that Bezalel was filled "with the Spirit of God in wisdom, in understanding, in knowledge, *and in all kinds of craftmanship*" (v. 3, emphasis added). This supernatural empowerment was for the purpose of making "artistic designs for work in gold, in silver, and in bronze, and in the cutting of stones for settings, and in the carving of wood, that he may work in all kinds of craftmanship" (vv. 4-5). Bezalel received a divine impartation for architectural design and engineering execution. God also appointed Oholiab to work alongside Bezalel in addition to putting skill "in the hearts of *all* who are skillful" (v. 6, emphasis added). According to this verse, what artisans eventually produced with their hands was a reflection of something greater that God had deposited *in their hearts*.

This kind of empowerment, or anointing, was not an isolated case. Noah received a special anointing to build the ark, an unprecedented assignment. Joseph received one to run the Egyptian empire. Moses received one to lead the people of Israel through the wilderness. Joshua received several to take Jericho and the Promised Land. Daniel received one to be the prime minister of Babylon. And Nehemiah received one to repair the wall.

Each of these people operated at a level of supernatural efficiency made possible only by the Spirit of God that was in them. This same power is available to you today. If you have failed in the marketplace, it could be because you did not rely on God but on your own understanding.

You must tackle the job at hand in the power of the Holy Spirit. He is the One who will lead you to all truth and justice. The Holy Spirit is the ultimate competitive advantage. He is the insider who can give you tips. He is the best hedge you have for your capital. When He gives you counsel, you need to take it. When you get in trouble, He is there to get you out of it.

The Power of Integrity

Before working in the health-care industry, I was on the fast-track for a management position at an international hotel in Argentina. My boss and the people I worked with knew about my Christian standards, but from time to time I took serious abuse from them. One of those instances happened in the context of a secret in-house rule that made me very uncomfortable. It specified that when Americans placed a call to the United States, we were required to overcharge them substantially. This was before computerized phones and billing systems became available, so the opportunity for overcharging was there.

I found myself caught between this rule and my Christian principles, so I avoided taking any phone-call requests. But one day I could not evade taking one. All of a sudden my colleagues' eyes were riveted on me, wondering what was I going to do. When I told them that I would charge the exact amount, a female employee, who was also the boss's mistress, warned me that she would turn me in. With a smirk she added, "And you know that the boss likes me more than he likes you." Nonetheless, I did the right thing.

Two hours later a human tornado burst into my office: my boss. He was so angry and out of control that his face looked totally distorted. It was as if demons were coming out of every pore of his body. Without any preamble he unleashed a relentless tirade of brutal verbal abuse. He called me every bad name in the book plus some new ones that he made up on the spot. While trying to cope with this cannonade of abuse, I found myself quietly crying out to the Holy Spirit for help. I remembered the promise that He would be with me always.

With eyes flaming mercilessly, through clenched teeth he fumed, "Why did you disobey my order?" Unexpectedly I found myself saying something that the Holy Spirit had sovereignly put in my mouth. I calmly responded, "Sir, if I am willing to risk my position by refusing to steal from an American who will never know what I did for him, can you imagine how much more certain you can be that I will never steal from you?" The logic of the argument was devastating. Only the Holy Spirit could have come up with something like that under the circumstances.

There was nothing my boss could say. He turned around and left, slamming the door so hard that it almost came off the hinges. However, three hours later he invited me to dinner. He made no reference to the incident that afternoon, but dinner was his way of apologizing. Not too long afterward I joined the management team. The lesson in this is that the Holy Spirit is with you in your job, and His power and His gifts are ready to operate anytime, especially when you do not know what to do next. When you rely wholeheartedly on Him and His power, you steer clear from ineffectiveness and from the receiver, because no one is wiser than your spiritual legal counsel, the Holy Spirit.

Spiritual Deadlock

Deadlock among board members in a corporation occurs when two opposing views are equal in strength. The opposing views may be excellent, but if they cause deadlock, they become detrimental because the board needs to be able to move things forward.

In the spirit realm deadlock takes place when two good things of similar value oppose and neutralize each other. An area where this is most likely to happen is the one involving traditional pastors and marketplace ministers. Earlier in this book I explained that both groups have valid and interdependent calls. Church-growth expert C. Peter Wagner makes a distinction between the molecular church and the extended church, explaining that traditional pastors serve in the *molecular church* and marketplace

Christians in the *extended church*, but both serve *in* the Church.

Traditional pastors are already recognized as ministers. The challenge before us today is how to acknowledge marketplace ministers as ministers *and* peers. This requires the resolution of three major issues: the first one has to do with differences in worldview, the second with expected levels of involvement and the third with the need for intentional reconciliation.

An Expanded Worldview

Marketplace Christians are most likely to have a more comprehensive and integrated view of society than traditional ministers have. To them the different components that make possible life in the city are interrelated and must be treated accordingly. To people in the marketplace, theology is something that needs to affect every social component in a practical and tangible way. Traditional pastors, by virtue of their professional training, tend to see society through a vertical theological grid that is less connected to the horizontal dimension of everyday situations. They are usually clear in their understanding of where society should go but less precise on *how* to get there. This is true especially of Caucasian pastors in the Western world and is why issues related to social action, civil rights and marketplace justice rate comparatively lower with them.

In October 2001, *Charisma* published an article titled "Impacting Our Culture," which featured four extremely successful ministries that are radically transforming neighborhoods and beginning to have an impact on cities in America. These ministries are doing more than simply caring for homeless people; they are effectively revitalizing the local economy, feeding the hungry, teaching the illiterate, identifying and training future entrepreneurs, launching local businesses and much more. In fact, in a few cases the ministries are transforming all aspects of life in their sphere of influence.[2] Interestingly, these four ministries are led by African-American pastors. Ministry in the inner city is not the province of a particular ethnic group. In cities all over America there are wonderful ministries that focus on the poor and are led by Hispanics, Asians, Caucasians, African-Americans and others. However, the question I wish to address here is, Why are these four unusual and very successful ministries led by African-Americans?

The reason, it seems to me, is that pastors in the African-American culture have traditionally been deeply involved in social issues. During slavery the pastor was usually the most educated black person around. This made him the spokesperson for his people: the workers, the families, the youth and the businessmen in his congregation. It is no wonder that the civil rights movement in the '60s was led by African-American pastors. To them the issues were not theological in the abstract sense of the word but very practical. They did not stand up just in support of church issues but in defense of African-American society. To them justice is not justice until it becomes *social* justice. Martin Luther King, Jr., saw social justice as a most necessary manifestation of divine justice, as an expression of God's will *on Earth.*

In general, I have found that committed marketplace Christians are closer in societal outlook to African-American pastors than to white pastors who tend to be more focused on vertical issues. This is a personal observation of mine devoid of any moral judgment. I am simply trying to show how historical roots affect our contemporary view of society. To Christian businesspeople the different components of the marketplace are vital and rate very high on their priority list. Whatever theology they are exposed to needs to affect those components or it will become irrelevant. In that sense they are no different than African-American pastors who see themselves connected to every component in society through the people they minister to in their congregations.

A person's worldview is the grid through which he or she sees and processes the reality in which he or she lives. For pulpit and marketplace ministers to be able to understand each and eventually work together in a harmonious and efficient way, they need to be aware of their differences on this point. If they are not, then some form of deadlock will occur: Marketplace Christians will not be released to do Church in the marketplace. And traditional pastors will fail miserably when they try to integrate marketplace people into the mainstream of church life.

Levels of Involvement for Marketplace Christians

There are some lessons in ethnic reconciliation that can be helpful when trying to integrate marketplace ministers and traditional pastors. The fact that today nonwhites are welcome to participate in Caucasian activities represents a major breakthrough from the pre-Civil-Rights-movement days. Caucasians, especially older ones, tend to congratulate themselves on how open-minded they are for welcoming nonwhites into their circle but often fail to think of anything beyond participation. However, nonwhites see participation as just an entry level. They aspire to much more. They want partnership and eventually leadership. This, of course, has begun to happen in some places since the 1960s and the advances made through the Civil Rights movement, but nonwhites aspire to much more.

It is not enough to allow marketplace ministers to participate in ministry. They need to become ministry peers.

This aspiration for more than a basic level of involvement also applies to marketplace ministers in their relationship to pastors. It is not enough to allow marketplace ministers to *participate* in ministry. They need to become ministry *peers*. Furthermore, they should have a similar right to become partners. Ultimately, they must be welcome to lead. Obviously, in the same fashion that not every believer is a pastor, neither is every Christian called to serve in the marketplace as a spiritual leader, but those who are leaders need to be recognized. How to resolve this should become clear after we have considered the issue of reconciliation.

SUPERNATURAL RECONCILIATION

There is an urgent need for reconciliation between traditional pastors and marketplace Christians for spiritual deadlock to be avoided, or eliminated, depending upon the case. Tension between these two groups is not new. In the New Testament we read of Alexander the coppersmith, obviously a businessman, who caused Paul, a minister, many troubles (see 1 Tim. 1:20; 2 Tim. 4:14). We also read of Diotrephes, who used his position as an elder to impose his will on others in order to shut out the apostle John (see

3 John 9). These two represent bad examples, Alexander of a marketplace Christian and Diotrephes of a local church leader, who used their positions to bring division instead of reconciliation.

Pastors have hurt marketplace leaders, albeit unwillingly and often unknowingly. The impression has been given that marketplace people are not spiritual enough. As noted earlier, the most common put-down among them is "I am just a layperson." It falls to the pastors to deal with the situation, and more often than not they have not met the problem head-on. The elders in a church have also wounded pastors, especially once they have attained positions of leadership on the board of elders. It is not uncommon to hear an elder say, "Pastors are so heavenly minded that they are no earthly good." There must be reconciliation between the two.

The challenge at hand is no different from the one faced by pastors and intercessors in the early 1980s. At that time, generally speaking, intercessors felt ignored and in some cases despised by pastors. They knew they had a call, but time and again they were denied a place at the table. On the other hand, pastors felt abused and in some cases manipulated by intercessors. They welcomed the idea of having more prayer incorporated into the spiritual menu, but too often after talking to intercessors they were left feeling unspiritual. Today, in general, pastors and intercessors work together very well. The road leading to the current harmony has three major milestones.

First, in the same fashion that today the Scriptures are being illuminated and long-neglected insights are coming to light to explain the value and the role of marketplace Christians, in the 1980s a steady flow of biblical teaching validated intercession. The first step now is to affirm the biblical legitimacy of Christianity in the marketplace and the role of marketplace Christians in the expansion of the kingdom of God.

Second, pastors need to extend the right hand of fellowship to marketplace Christians. In the same fashion that because rich people are in control of the resources, they need to reach out to the poor, traditional pastors need to reach out to marketplace Christians. Rich Marshall, author of God@Work, did this in his own church. He organized an ordination service for marketplace Christians in which he and the elders commissioned business, education and government leaders.

Third, both groups have to be integrated and work as such. Ministerial prayer meetings need to include marketplace Christians. City-reaching thrusts must have them on board as well. Given the freshness of these concepts there is no road map to lead us, but we must try. In Spanish we have a saying, *Camino se hace al andar*, which means, "You build the road as you walk." If we do, I am confident that 10 years from now marketplace Christians will be fully integrated into the mainstream of ministry, very much like what happened with intercessors.

A Spiritual Business Plan

Consider the following five-step spiritual reorganization plan, which includes prayer, to deal with deception, inefficiency and deadlock:

1. Discard the *deception* that you are not a minister. Let the wealth of truth in the Word of God wash away all unbiblical distortions regarding your *identity* and your *calling*. Agree with God that you are a minister called to the marketplace.

   Father God, I declare that I am Your workmanship, created in Christ Jesus unto good works in the marketplace. This is my destiny and this is my place of ministry. I accept Your call and I commit to faithfully walk in it from now on.

2. Reject the *deception* that your job in the marketplace is nonspiritual. Labor becomes worship when it is done unto the glory of God. Your job is the vehicle to take care of God's creation and bring the kingdom of God to those with whom you work. Renounce any negative notion that labels your job as unworthy or unspiritual.

   Father God, I bless my job in the name of the Lord Jesus. I repent of all negative thoughts, words spoken and actions taken by me against my job. From now on I will consider work my ministry and ministry my work, and I will do everything unto the glory of God so that my labor will constitute an act of worship.

3. Officially welcome the Lord Jesus into your workplace for His perfect *efficiency* to replace your own deficiency or insufficiency. Literally go to the front door, open it and say, "Welcome, Lord Jesus. Come in. I need You." Then walk with Him all over the place. As you do, talk to Jesus about every person with whom you work.

Lord Jesus, I have heard You knocking on the door of my work and I now open the door for You to come in. Thank You that as I do this, You do come in. I recognize that until now I have been wretched, miserable, poor, blind and naked. But now I have invited You to come in to have fellowship (dinner). Such fellowship will transform, restore, enrich, enlighten and clothe me spiritually. Thank You, Lord Jesus, that You are here to stay!

4. Select a place at work to serve as a symbolic altar. It does not have to be religious in appearance. In my case, it was the Jesus chair (see chapter 2). Make it your Bethel, a location where you meet with God and His angels minister to you. His wisdom will increase your *efficiency*, and His angels will protect you from evil.

Holy Spirit, I come to You to be filled with Your presence. I also pray for spiritual gifts to be activated in me and for You to grant me the fullness of Your power to use them in my job, which is my ministry. I also welcome Your ministering angels to stand guard over this outpost of ministry in the marketplace.

5. The Father rules supreme over the earth. Jesus is the head of the Church, and the Holy Spirit is leading it to all truth and righteousness. In fact, the Trinity rules over the whole world. Your job should not be the exception. Recognize the Trinity as the head of the corporation where you work. Acknowledge the Father as the chairman of the board, Jesus as the CEO and the Holy Spirit as the legal counsel. Proclaim their supreme superiority over you so that *deadlock* will never again be a possibility.

Holy Trinity, Father, Son and Holy Spirit, let this corporation be the place of Your habitation. May Your presence fill every aspect of it and may Your eternal purposes be carried out in every detail and at every level so that the kingdom of God will be in evidence in my work and that eventually the whole earth will hear Your voice. Amen.

Notes

1. *Merriam-Webster's Collegiate Dictionary*, 10th ed., s.v. "inefficient."
2. Adrienne S. Gaines, "The Church That Changed a City," *Charisma* (October 2001), p. 50. For more information about specific ministries that have begun to move in this way, see *Christianity Today* (October 2001) and Continental's *In-Flight* (October 2001).

DOING
BUSINESS
GOD'S WAY

We draw our strength from the battle. From our greatest
conflicts come our greatest victories!

ROD PARSLEY

Now that you have rededicated yourself to God and embraced your destiny in the marketplace, you must begin to walk in this newness of life. To do this effectively it will be helpful to understand that there are different manifestations and seasons for the anointing. Anointing is simply God's empowerment to do His work so that the will of God will be done on Earth.

ANOINTING IN THE BIBLE

David's Anointing

When Samuel anointed David to be king over an entire nation, very few people knew about it. Nevertheless, for several years David knew deep down that he was destined to be king, even though the circumstances around him were not at all royal. This may be your case. Perhaps you are still in school, out of work or in a difficult position, but deep down you know that God has anointed you for ministry in the marketplace. You also know that it is for something significant in God's eyes. Hang on to the vision while you quietly prepare for the day when it will become evident to everyone who needs to know. Faith is the manifestation of things hoped for (see Heb. 11:1). If the seed is already in you, then so is the potential for the tree and the fruit.

Back in the 1990s an employee of the Argentine prison system drove me from La Plata to San Nicolas. As the car went by a certain prison, he pointed to it and declared, "One day I will run a prison." I asked him why was he so sure, and he replied, "Because the Lord told me so." Even though he was just a prison employee, in his heart he was *already* the warden of a prison because faith is the manifestation of things for which we hope. Sure enough, fewer than five years later he became the warden of a large prison. As soon as he took over, he made it a priority to implement biblical principles among the guards and inmates. Soon that particular prison became one of the best in Argentina.

This man had an anointing similar to the one David had. Only he, God and a few people knew that he was destined to run a prison. Such conviction led him to carry out every work assignment with that goal in mind. Whether he was cleaning up a room or walking an inmate to meet with a lawyer, in his mind he was running the prison. This, in turn, allowed him to bring a dimension of excellence to his job that did not escape the attention of his superiors.

If you know what God has in store for you, begin to act on it right away. Today you may not be a manager or the CEO of your company. You may have a very low position, but if you know that God has anointed you for business, He will keep expanding your sphere of influence until you reach the level He has chosen for you (see Prov. 22:29; Matt. 25:23). The key is not to let circumstances conspire against what God has told you and not to let them prevent you from believing that His will shall come to pass. Joseph behaved in jail with the same solicitousness as if he were already walking the halls of the royal palace.

So often, people called to ministry in the marketplace find themselves in an unappealing spot. Because of their call they think that they need to quit their jobs and go to seminary in order to fulfill it. Dennis Doyle, president of Welsh Companies, a very large commercial real estate company in the United States, felt that way after coming to Argentina to attend one of Harvest Evangelism's conferences. God touched him, and he thought that the way to respond was to quit his position in the marketplace. God used people and circumstances to show him a more excellent way. He stayed in business, expanded his corporation and, along with his wife, Megan, and other Christian businesspeople birthed Nehemiah Partners, a ministry to Christians in the marketplace. Dennis and his associates have been instrumental in equipping Christians to make the marketplace their parish.

If you find yourself in a similar spot, do not rush. Do the best you can with what you have got while you wait for God to break through, just like David did. Rich Marshall, whose book *God@Work* is an excellent tool to help Christians find their destiny in the marketplace, was instrumental in encouraging Dennis to stay in the marketplace.[1]

David's anointing was a kingly anointing. Today this anointing is given to those who are called to exercise significant leadership in the marketplace, even in the nation. The point I am making here is that people with this anointing should never let contradictory circumstances prevent them from persevering in their quest. God will come through. As we will see later, there is also an anointing for people who are called to serve in less visible but equally important positions.

Esther's Anointing

Esther was married to a powerful Gentile king. It was not the kind of marriage that she or her cousin, who was also her guardian, had envisioned, but she had no choice in the matter (see Esther 2:1-8). Nonetheless, she decided to make the most of the situation.

First, she recognized that her husband had a position given by God and chose to honor it by serving him and giving him marital pleasure. When she felt that she had something urgent to say to him, she did not just blurt it out (see Esther 5:7-8). She patiently waited for the right moment, and when it came, the results were extraordinary. Esther and her cousin, Mordecai, were empowered by the king when he realized the value of their service to him and to the kingdom (see Esther 8:7-14).

If you are married to someone who works in the marketplace, even to one who is not walking with the Lord as he or she should, take note of this particular anointing. When you protect your spouse with your prayers, taking care of him or her and waiting on God for the perfect moment to share wisdom, you will be empowering his or her position in the marketplace. And when this happens, you and your family will reap the benefits, just as Esther and her family did.

Priscilla and Aquila's Anointing

Priscilla was a businesswoman who, unlike Esther, partnered with her husband, Aquila, in both business and ministry. She was very knowledgeable in the things of God. In fact, she knew so much that when the time came for Apollos to be instructed further as far as doctrine is concerned, she played a very active part in it. Luke lists her before Aquila, which could indicate that she was the lead teacher (see Acts 18:24-28). This is not necessarily out of order, because man's headship should not preclude the wife from taking leadership in a specific field if she is more qualified and if she does it in the proper way—with his full blessing. Earlier, when Luke referred to the two by their trade, Aquila is the one who is listed first, probably because in business he was the lead person (see Acts 18:1-3).

I know a married couple who are the modern equivalent of Priscilla and Aquila. They are Larry and Rose Ihle, who own Dexterity Dental Arts, Inc., a dental laboratory located in a suburb of Minneapolis, Minnesota.

When they bought out their original partner, they recognized that God had called them to be the pastors over their corporation. As part of this role they pray for every employee, vendor and client on a regular basis. As a result, they have seen the kingdom of God defeat and evict evil influences. Their prayer meetings are open to all employees, and many attend. In fact, some of them have experienced miracles. They tithe from the income of the corporation as well as their personal income. But above everything else, they hear from God concerning their business affairs. On one hand they run their business according to biblical principles with which they are familiar. On the other hand, they expect God to speak to them as the need arises. God is indeed the chairman of the board, Jesus the CEO and the Holy Spirit the legal counsel of Dexterity Dental Arts, Inc. The Ihles travel all over the world inspiring other marketplace Christians and showing them how to do business God's way instead of man's way.

Not satisfied, they also take the kingdom of God to folks in the town where their laboratory is located. The week before Thanksgiving in 2001, Larry, with Rose's prayer support, loaded trailers with $10,000 worth of top-of-the-line food (steak, fish, chicken, etc.) and distributed it to the poor in the neighborhoods around their factory. Because there was a lot of food left, Larry decided to distribute it in nearby bars, since that was a place where people could be found.

On the way to the first bar Larry picked up a man who was known as a heavy drinker and asked him to come along, since the man knew the patrons very well. Larry also prayed for him, specifically asking God to heal the tip of his finger that had been cut with a band saw and was in great pain. As Larry and the man came into the bar, Larry introduced himself to the owner, prayed for him and asked his permission to make an announcement that free food was available in his truck outside. People helped themselves to food while Larry prayed for them.

In the meantime, Larry's impromptu assistant was dramatically healed of his finger injury, to the point that new skin instantly grew over the wound. He got so excited that he grabbed a stack of gospel tracts and began to distribute them to his drinking buddies while giving testimony of the power of God. Two people received the Lord right there.

Larry and his assistant drove to a second bar where they did the same, and three more people received the Lord. From there they proceeded to a third bar where seven others accepted Christ as Savior. The ace up Larry's sleeve was his assistant, who vehemently validated Larry's words by pointing to his healed finger and enthusiastically passing out gospel tracts. As a result of this outreach, Larry is regularly going back to these bars to bring the kingdom of God to the patrons, very much the way Jesus did in the Gospels.

It could be that you are a modern Priscilla or Aquila. If you and your spouse have a common call to ministry, your relationship becomes crucial. My friend and colleague Jack Serra, in his book *Marketplace, Marriage and Revival: The Spiritual Connection,* has very helpful insights on how to protect this kind of marriage in order to be able to successfully merge business and ministry.[2]

Lydia's Anointing

As I noted earlier in this book, the first European convert was a businesswoman named Lydia. She dealt in purple fabrics—very expensive materials. Apparently she made a very good living because she owned a home in Philippi where she conducted business and most likely also owned one in Thyatira, where she was from. Luke reports that she was a very determined person who prevailed upon Paul and his band to stay at her house. She must have been fearless also, because the newly established church met in her home while Paul and Silas were in jail (see Luke 16:14-15,40). How many people do you know who will open up their home to members of a newly formed group considered illegal by the authorities? This happens in China but rarely anyplace else. This lady had guts!

We know that Lydia had a family, because Luke refers to her household (see Acts 16:15). However, since no mention is made of her husband, perhaps she was a widow who still had children living at home. She was energetic, successful and wealthy. She was also very godly, because she is described as a worshiper of God whose heart was opened by God to respond to the message preached by Paul (see Acts 16:11-15).

If you find that Lydia's profile matches yours, most likely you have an anointing similar to hers. A woman can be strong and remain feminine. She can be a wise leader and godly at the same time. In my book *Women: God's Secret Weapon*, I discuss at length the extraordinary role of women in God's kingdom due to the unique way in which they have been designed.[3] But you do not have to be a woman to have the Lydia anointing.

For years Pat and Shirley Boone opened up their Beverly Hills home for Bible studies for people in the entertainment industry. Pat had been one of the most popular pop singers in the early 1960s and had built a solid reputation as a marketplace Christian. As a result, nonbelievers and people in show business who were not comfortable in traditional church settings would come; many were saved and many were baptized in the Boones' swimming pool. Pat Boone tells the story of one miracle after another in his autobiography, *A New Song*.[4]

> A woman can be strong and remain feminine. She can be a wise leader and godly at the same time.

Boone's reputation in the entertainment marketplace is so strong that in 2001, when Larry King did a television talk show on miracles, he invited Boone to be a guest. On that day, millions of King's viewers heard about the power of prayer.

You do not have to be famous or wealthy to move in this anointing. In the early 1970s, Al Merrick started a small surfboard manufacturing business just outside Santa Barbara, California. From the start Al dedicated his work to God, prayed over each board he made and inscribed Scriptures on them. Before long, some of the best surfers in the world were knocking at his door, and Al became known as a premiere surfboard shaper. When someone showed up at Al's shop, before he would talk about surfboards, often he would open up the Scriptures and talk about Jesus. Al and his wife welcomed people into their home for Bible studies, inviting surfers from local beaches, and they ran a Jesus People coffeehouse.

Today, Merrick's Channel Islands Surfboards is the largest surfboard manufacturing company in the world. The business is still dedicated to God, and Al's son, Britt, has followed in his father's footsteps. Britt, who has created his own line of surfboards, has also taken up a mantle in ministry. One of the first things Britt did after he rededicated his life to God was go to a local beach and invite surfers over to his house for a Bible study. Most of those kids accepted Jesus. Britt used his family's marketplace reputation to gain a foothold to share the gospel and to see God transform lives.

Not only does Britt continue to work at Channel Islands as a marketplace Christian, but today he is also an associate pastor at Calvary Chapel, Santa Barbara, leads a Friday-night outreach popular with surfers, and ministers at surfing competitions. Britt's influence goes deep into the surfing community. He has received reports of surfers on far-flung beaches around the world who have been listening to his Bible-teaching tapes; and not too long ago, a few nights before Halloween, Britt ran into a world-ranked surfer on the streets of Santa Barbara. That surfer, who was ready for a night of partying, came to Britt's meeting instead and tearfully responded to an altar call. That professional surfer then went out and invited to church some of the friends with whom he would have partied.

In the cases of the Boones and the Merricks, they not only are great examples of marketplace Christians, but they also have shown how marketplace evangelism can penetrate subcultures that have been resistant to traditional methods.

The Little Servant's Anointing

After going through the previous roster of anointings you may feel left out because you are not at the level of the people I discussed. You are not a corporate CEO, a high-ranking government official, a celebrity or world-class surfer. Perhaps you are a small-business owner, a lower-ranking employee or a servant.

If this is your situation, then you are entitled to the servant's anointing. Before I delve into the details of this anointing, it is important to remember that from God's perspective, the word "servant" is not a pejorative term. In fact, this is how many of the apostles—Paul, James, Peter, Jude and John—proudly introduced themselves (see Rom. 1:1; Jas. 1:1; 2 Peter 1:1; Jude 1:1; Rev. 1:1). Mary, the greatest woman who ever lived, described herself as a servant (see Luke 1:38). Most important of all, Jesus is presented as the servant par excellence (see Acts 3:13,26; 4:27,30; Phil. 2:7).

God has a very high view of servants. Jesus said, "Well done, good and faithful servant! You have been faithful in a few things; I will put you in charge of many things. Come and share your master's happiness" (Matt. 25:23, *NIV*). In fact, only servants are entrusted with the opportunity to move from "a few things" to "many things" simply because of their faithfulness. In addition, they are promised that they will share in their master's happiness. This is indeed a very special anointing.

The prototype for this anointing is found in the book of 2 Kings (see 5:1-5), where we find the story of a high-ranking official in Aram. He was a victorious general, a great man, highly respected by the king. In one of his military missions he brought home a little girl from the land of Israel. She was a captive, and he assigned her to wait upon his wife.

It is unlikely that your position is as low as that of this girl who had been forcefully removed from her family and country and turned into a slave. She was a little girl, but she had a great destiny. She told her mistress that she knew how the

> Only servants are entrusted with the opportunity to move from "a few things" to "many things" simply because of their faithfulness.

master of the house could find divine healing. Obviously her words were timely *and anointed,* because they were relayed first to the general and then to the king himself. This resulted in the eventual healing of the general and also in his conversion to the little girl's God. I know this is the case because he promised Elisha that he will "not sacrifice to other gods, but to the Lord" (2 Kings 5:17). This was not meant to be a one-time occurrence, because he also asked Elisha for God to pardon him when he was required to go into the temple of a pagan god as part of his official duties. None of this would have happened without *the little servant girl.* She was used to change a powerful man who in turn influenced a powerful nation.

If this picture matches who you are and where you are in the marketplace, take heart. You may not be destined to rise to the top, but you are anointed to minister to those at the top and through them change things all around. It is important to influence the top influencers because they are the ones who hold the keys to society, for better or for worse. In the Bible, when the king sought God, the nation was blessed. The opposite was also true: The sins of the king quickly defiled the nation.

God always places humble people such as this little girl in close proximity to powerful people to accomplish His purposes. It is wise to remember that the Iron Curtain was not brought down in 1990 by armies or by a nuclear bomb. It came down thanks to the quiet influence of a very humble woman on Mikhail Gorbachev, the leader of the former U.S.S.R. This woman was his mother, a believer in the Lord Jesus Christ, who planted in young Mikhail's mind seeds impregnated with the Word of God. When the moment came to bring about the most extraordinary social event of the twentieth century, it was those seeds that gave Gorbachev the courage to proceed.

Whether you are a modern David, Esther, Priscilla, Aquila, Lydia or little servant girl, recognize that God has anointed you for ministry in the marketplace and that such an anointing must be used in the power of the Holy Spirit. Flowing in that anointing will protect you from deceit, inefficiency and spiritual deadlock.

A Contemporary Example of a Marketplace Christian

Earlier I wrote about how it is not enough to be a Christian in the marketplace. We need to do business God's way with the clear intent to see the marketplace transformed. Let me describe a contemporary example of someone who is doing just that.

His dad was a tailor. He grew up in a poor neighborhood where weekly homicides were the norm. Along with his family, he was the target of racism and prejudice. But his parents were believers who made sure he grew up in church. He got good grades in school and eventually graduated from a prestigious college, landing an important job on Wall Street.

He did well there, but ultimately he felt the call to pastoral ministry. He went back to school, obtained a degree in theology and, after serving in various pulpits, took over a congregation of 25 members in a deprived, violent area of town, not unlike the one he grew up in.

Today his church has 14,000 members and runs a center for victims of HIV. He also built a 104,000-square-foot commercial center that employs 276 people, houses a community college, has office space for small businesses and is home to a bank. In less than two years this center, three miles from his church, has had a $28.7-million economic impact on its immediate surroundings. As a result what used to be a pathetic area of town has now been revitalized and several national chains have set up shop there. At present he is developing a community which comprises 452 single-family homes, a wellness center for drug-addicted mothers to be able to stay with their children while detoxifying themselves, a 166,000-square-foot family life center, a park, sports facilities and a retirement community. He believes unapologetically that Christians should succeed financially in order to do God's work. In his own words he expresses why we need many Zacchaeuses around: "It's unfortunate that most spiritual church folk don't have a lot of financial resources. What this society needs, among other things, are more spiritual folks with resources. What that would mean is they would understand that their prosperity has a purpose and that God has given them the power to get wealth so that they can use it for the Kingdom."[5]

Who is this man? His name is Kirbyjon Caldwell. An article in *Christianity Today* described him as "megachurch pastor, real estate whiz, community developer, and the president's spiritual adviser."[6]

Most Americans got a good glance at him on their television screens when he prayed for President George W. Bush at his inauguration on January 20, 2000. It was a most unusual prayer. After asking for God's favor to be on the president and his wife, Caldwell intoned, "We decree and declare that no weapon formed against them shall prosper." A definite first for prayers said at a presidential inauguration.

This example epitomizes marketplace transformation. The son of a tailor, raised in a deprived neighborhood, now brings spiritual and economic transformation to people and neighborhoods. He also embodies the fulfillment of the biblical truth that a man who is diligent in his work will stand before kings (see Prov. 22:29).

When he launched his career, Kirbyjon Caldwell did not set out to do everything he is doing today. When he went to school, he did not have a blueprint for the rest of his life. In fact, he became a businessman but left that profession to become a pastor. Yet he eventually returned to his business roots and connected them with his ministry. I am sure he must have filed for spiritual Chapter 11 more than once. And every time he did, he came out stronger. Today he is eloquently demonstrating that Church is business—God's business as Jesus called it (see Luke 3:49)—and that business can be church when Church happens in the marketplace.

GO FOR IT!

In the preceding pages you have read about people such as the Boones, the Merricks, the Ihles, Rick Heeren, Dave Wendorff, Charity Wallace, Vaughn MacLaughlin, Kirbyjon Caldwell, Joey (the jeepney driver in the Philippines) and many others. All of them have inspired you with their testimonies, I am sure. The key to their successes is twofold: They recognized that they have been anointed for business (destiny), and they decided to move in that anointing (obedience). The rest was entirely up to God.

Paul, the premier example of a marketplace Christian, wrote to the Corinthians that in their case he planted and Apollos watered, but it was God who caused the seed to grow (see 1 Cor. 3:3-5). Only God can produce results—growth. However, such growth is dependent on our obedience to be willing to plant and to water the seed entrusted to us.

You are anointed for business—God's business. Your job is your pulpit, and the marketplace is your parish. You have been called by God to bring His kingdom to the marketplace. Who you are and what you have been entrusted with are not issues. Both have been decided already by God Himself. The question is whether or not you are going to take the first step of obedience and begin to move in the anointing.

I have three words of very simple advice: Go for it!

Notes

1. Rich Marshall, *God@Work* (Shippensberg, PA: Destiny Image, 1999).
2. Jack Serra, *Marketplace, Marriage and Revival: The Spiritual Connection* (Orlando, FL: Longwood Communications, 2001).
3. Ed Silvoso, *Women: God's Secret Weapon* (Ventura, CA: Regal Books, 2001).
4. Pat Boone, *A New Song* (Lake Mary, FL: Creation House, n.d.). This book is currently out of print, but it is worth reading if you can find a copy.
5. Jenny Staff Johnson, "The Minister of Good Success," *Christianity Today* (October 2001), n.p.
6. Ibid.

ANOINTED FOR BUSINESS

STUDY GUIDE

FOR PERSONAL OR SMALL-GROUP STUDY

How to Use the
Study Guide

The purpose of this study guide is to highlight key points in *Anointed for Business* and to lead you to make personal application of the information you receive. It is divided into the following sections:

- **Section A: Study Guide**—highlights key points of each chapter and serves as a study guide and review (an answer key is in the back).
- **Section B: Reflection and Discussion**—for personal reflection and/or discussion within a group reading the book together.
- **Section C: My Journal**—for you to record your personal thoughts or what the Holy Spirit speaks to you.

At the end of this study guide is a **Personal Application** to help you set challenging commitments. The practical, everyday implementation of biblical principles in the marketplace by marketplace Christians is a deciding factor for marketplace transformation. Consider the pages in this personal application section as the culmination of this study and an essential component in your destiny as a person who is anointed for business.

The Personal Application Section is divided into three parts. Section I, "My Spiritual Business Plan," and Section II, "My Path to Marketplace Reconciliation," suggest ways that you can implement what you have read in *Anointed for Business*. Use Section III to review the commitments you make, see personal progress, and recommit to God's course of action for your life and business.

May the Lord bless and guide you as you read and implement what He reveals to you through *Anointed for Business*.

FACILITATING AN
ANOINTED FOR BUSINESS
SMALL GROUP

We encourage you to find a few others to read or listen to *Anointed for Business* along with you. Suggested components of a one-hour meeting are as follows:

- Group comes having read or listened to assigned chapter(s) and having filled in the Section A study guide questions (use answer key if necessary).
- Leader facilitates discussion using Section B for about 30 minutes.
- For the remaining time, members pray for each other's felt needs and the needs of their businesses, expecting marketplace miracles in answer to those prayers.

INTRODUCTION

A. Study Guide

1. Three basic components of the marketplace are _____
   _____,
   _____, and
   _____.

2. Early Christians made the marketplace the focal point of their ministry because they saw the marketplace as their _____
   _____ and their business
   as a _____.

3. What did Jerusalem and other cities experience at the hands of individuals not known for their religious acumen but for their roles in the marketplace? _____
   _____.

4. List four misbeliefs that usually neutralize God's calling on those anointed for marketplace ministry.

B. Reflection and Discussion

1. What are two of your earliest memories of the marketplace?

2. Have you, as a marketplace Christian, ever felt like a second-class citizen in the kingdom of God?

3. What new perspective did you receive on *the marketplace and the Early Church* from reading this chapter?

4. If you have ever told someone, "I'm *just* a layperson" or have had another person say this to you, what has been the context and how has it made you feel?

5. Explain how any of the four lethal misbeliefs (see pages 20-21) have neutralized God's anointing on your life for marketplace ministry.

C. My Journal

CHAPTER 1

CONFESSIONS OF
A CHRISTIAN
BUSINESSMAN

A. Study Guide
1. What does it mean to be anointed?

2. _____ anointing is not found in the Bible.

3. The level of anointing God has in mind for people in the market-place is meant to _____ people and their
_____.

4. Jesus' promise in Mark 16:17-18 (be filled with the Holy Spirit, cast out demons, make the sick well) primarily applies to ministry in the _____.

5. The _____ _____ must be the focus of the mission entrusted to us, not just a church building or a gathering of believers.

B. Reflection and Discussion
1. Have you been told or have you considered, "Leave everything and go into the ministry"? Why?

2. Where do you believe the power God has given to us is to be primarily exercised? In the Church or in the marketplace? Defend your answer with Scripture.

3. What is the most you have hoped for in your role as a businessperson? Why?

C. My Journal

C H A P T E R   2

JESUS AND THE MARKETPLACE

A. Study Guide

1. Joseph and Jesus were more than simple woodworkers; they were

   _____.

2. What are two possible reasons why Jesus was born in a place of business?

3. Jesus can be seen as a profitable _____, a well-informed _____, a marketplace _____, and a performer of _____ miracles.

4. Describe Jesus' daily routine for most of His adult life.

5. What are a few examples Jesus used in His teaching that show He was familiar with the marketplace and its operation?

6. What was Jesus' financial status?

7. _____, in the Bible, is never presented as nonspiritual. In fact, labor is _____.

B. Reflection and Discussion

1. Have you pictured Jesus more as a monk or a manager? Explain.

2. What was your view of Jesus and His view of the marketplace prior to reading this chapter? How has it changed?

C. My Journal

THE DISCIPLES AND THE MARKETPLACE

A. Study Guide

1. All the disciples were _____ people, and the writing of the Gospels was entrusted to _____ leaders.

2. The first Christians were comfortable in _____ settings, were notable as the _____ of the Early Church, were capable of _____ and business, were excellent _____, and understood _____ truths.

3. The Church grew as recognized leaders were selected to _____ _____ with the apostles.

4. Most likely, the _____ prevented Early Christians from moving _____ as Jesus had specified. _____ forced the Church to move out of Jerusalem.

5. What happened as Paul and his coworkers began to focus on the marketplace?

6. Jesus Christ's design for the Church was to be the _____ _____, not another _____ merely satisfied with survival.

B. Reflection and Discussion

1. Have you seen working in the marketplace and serving in the Church as mutually exclusive activities? Explain.

2. How has the arbitrary classification of "full-time" and "part-time" ministry affected the Church?

3. Why do you believe Jesus intentionally chose marketplace people who were not members of the religious establishment?

C. My Journal

CHAPTER 4

THE GOD OF BUSINESS

A. Study Guide

1. The majority of the _____ _____ heroes were deeply involved in everyday _____ issues.

2. David did not believe that fighting Goliath was a _____ _____ enterprise and that running his business a _____ one. God was _____ in both of them.

3. The _____ _____ is to a businessperson what the _____ _____ _____ is to an athlete. With proper _____, it can benefit millions of people and can provide the incentive required for conquering exceptional _____.

4. What did David see about God and his job that allowed him to overcome his challenges?

5. We have wrongly dichotomized the _____ and _____ worlds.

6. Why is the devil afraid of marketplace Christians?

7. How does the devil try to disqualify marketplace Christians?

B. Reflection and Discussion

1. Why do you believe many marketplace Christians remain in business but give up on experiencing the joy of the Lord in their work or the joy of significant success?

2. Describe your own struggle with a fear of profit or of becoming materialistic.

3. Do you believe that the tangible world is intrinsically evil? Why or why not?

4. Have you considered that the devil may fear you as a marketplace Christian? What are some ways he has tried to prevent you from fulfilling your divine destiny in the marketplace?

5. Do you feel your work outside the Church is less spiritual than work done inside the Church?

6. What are some benefits when pastors and businesspeople relate as ministry peers?

C. My Journal

C H A P T E R   5

GOD LOVES
BILL GATES, TOO

A. Study Guide

1. What are two common misperceptions that often prevent godly Christians from moving enthusiastically into the marketplace?

2. Jesus was a friend of _____ sinners, _____ and _____ alike. He loved and ministered to _____.

3. Servants loyal to the returning King Jesus need to enter the _____ and use whatever He has entrusted to them to gain _____ through their _____.

4. What was the reward for business success that came about as a result of obedience?

5. Jesus understands both the rich and the poor because He fully _____ with each group.

6. Wealth has to be seen as a _____, and it has to be used _____ to _____ others as a practical expression of our belief that God is the _____ and the _____.

B. Reflection and Discussion

1. How does God really feel about the rich? Defend your answer with Scripture.

2. Describe your experience with the bias that ascribes virtue to poverty and innate evil to wealth (e.g., "it is better to be poor and godly than rich and worldly").

3. Re-read Luke 19:1-27. Discuss the misconceptions that Jesus wanted to correct by telling the parable of the 10 minas (see pages 68-69).

4. Is wealth a blessing or a curse? Read 1 Timothy 6:6-19 and discuss what Paul said is the problem and solution for those God has entrusted with riches (use pages 74-75 as a guide for the discussion if necessary).

C. My Journal

RECONCILIATION IN THE MARKETPLACE

A. Study Guide

1. What are the six social gaps that need to be bridged before the Church can confront the rulers of darkness over this world?

2. Where wealthy people in the Church shared their _____ and _____ with the poor, significant numbers of _____ were _____ to the Kingdom. In other words, there is a cause-and-effect dynamic between taking care of the _____ and spontaneous _____.

3. When the wealthy and the poor walk together, the rich provide _____ and the poor impart _____. When these come together, _____ soon becomes evident.

4. The Body of Christ grows _____. God will not allow one arm to be twice as long as the other.

B. Reflection and Discussion

1. How does reconciliation in the marketplace help the Church to attain a position from which it can wrestle spiritual control away from Satan and his wicked forces?

2. Like Jesus, Paul was a reconciler because he fully identified with both ends of the social spectrum. What are some practical ways the Church can truly and fully identify with both groups? (See pages 88-89.)

3. Is God leading you to take specific steps to forge a concrete path to reconciliation in the marketplace? Describe what you sense God may be saying to you. (Look at section 2 of the Personal Application section at the end of this guide.)

C. My Journal

CHAPTER 7

THE KINGDOM, THE CHURCH AND THE MARKETPLACE

A. Study Guide

1. The kingdom of God is intended to _____, not just individuals, but also the _____ and the _____ around them.

2. The kingdom of God existed _____, is coming _____ _____ _____ but is also for _____.

3. The kingdom of God is something _____ that has a deep effect on _____ _____.

4. The focus of the Church has been on bringing people into the church _____ instead of _____ _____ the kingdom of God to where the people are.

5. The Church is to be _____ and _____ rather than _____ and _____.

6. The Church exists to _____ and is _____ and _____ by the Lord to storm the gates of hell.

7. Who is "the Church"?

8. In the Early Church, the _____ became central to the Church's activities, especially _____ _____ endeavors.

9. Of the 40 major supernatural actions recorded in the book of Acts, 39 took place in the _____.

B. Reflection and Discussion

1. How has Satan's deception affected our understanding of the kingdom of God, the nature of the Church, and the Church's role in the marketplace? (See page 95.)

2. Why is the misbelief that the Church was born between four walls detrimental to our identity and our role in the Kingdom?

3. Why have Christians believed that the marketplace is less spiritual than a church?

4. In the story of Joe the Philippine taxi owner (see pages 106-107), Joe saw the church as a means to take the kingdom of God to people in the marketplace. Sinners came into the kingdom of God when they discovered that it had come near to them, and Joe taught them how to have church in the marketplace. What would it mean for you to have church in the marketplace? What obstacles might you face in this endeavor?

C. My Journal

CHAPTER 8

GOD IN THE BOARDROOM

A. Study Guide

1. The Church is the _____ and its members are the _____, but the market-place is the _____.

2. Marketplace Christians are operating their companies in a sub-standard manner because they are _____ the best-demonstrated practices of _____ companies.

3. If every believer will go to work fully convinced that he or she is _____ God through _____ and that every constructive action at work is a form of _____ _____, our cities would be transformed.

B. Reflection and Discussion

1. Look at the four levels of relationship a Christian has with the marketplace and their descriptions (see pages 110-111). Assess your present relationship with the marketplace according to this definition.

2. Share a story of God's power in your place of business as a result of prayer.

3. Stop and pray for a need you presently have, asking God to bring a breakthrough in the situation for the kingdom of God. Consider asking a few others to join you in prayer for this need on site at your place of business this week.

C. My Journal

CHAPTER 9

FOUR STEPS TO FINDING YOUR DESTINY IN THE MARKETPLACE

A. Study Guide

1. No matter where you find yourself in the marketplace today, what is important is that you _____ your calling to _____ that place by using the _____ that God has made available to you.

2. What was the fundamental difference between the Twelve and the Seventy that Jesus sent out in Luke 10?

3. What were the four steps that gave victory to the Seventy in Luke 10?

4. What is the marketplace version of these four actions?

5. When you make peace with your job, you _____ the evil elements that have created strife between you and your work. When you embrace it, you make it a part of your life that makes God's _____ extend to your job.

6. Nothing points marketplace people toward the Lord better than when they see a _____ in the marketplace.

7. _____ can always increase, but _____ can only decrease.

B. Reflection and Discussion

1. Review and discuss each of the four principles of Luke 10 as applied to the marketplace (see pages 125-130). What might each look like in your place of business?

2. Review and discuss the five levels of misery and comfort (see pages 132-134). Where do you find yourself most often? Take a moment to pray and ask God to plant in your heart faith to see the entire marketplace transformed in your city.

C. My Journal

YOUR DESTINY: SAVING THE NATION

A. Study Guide

1. _____ rates higher with God than our attempts at _____ the command He is giving us.

2. God is able to see us, not through the grim grid of past _____ _____, but through the pristine prism of the future _____ He has in store for us.

3. _____ in spite of _____ is what made Gideon such a hero.

4. If sin were able to do so much damage, _____ would definitely be capable of doing much more restoration, because where _____ abounds, _____ always overflows.

B. Reflection and Discussion

1. God always has a higher opinion of us than the one we have of ourselves. Stop and pray right now and ask God to show you what you look like through His eyes.

2. Using the life of Gideon as an example, what might God say if He appeared to you?

3. How does God's mandate to Adam and Eve in the Garden apply to His mandate for you in the marketplace? (See page 145.)

C. My Journal

WHY GOD WANTS YOU TO DECLARE CHAPTER 11 BANKRUPTCY

A. Study Guide

1. In the spiritual world, bankruptcy is the inability to _____ _____.

2. It is essential that you be transparent and examine yourself in the areas of _____, _____, or a _____.

3. Failing to be _____ with God and with each other causes us to _____ _____ and to be _____.

4. The wages of sin is _____. Sin is _____, _____ and _____. Yielding to sin drives you away from God, His _____, and _____. Because sin is so destructive, God will use whatever means to bring us to a point of _____.

5. _____ in the Scriptures is when we implement God's will on Earth, rather than try to subtract ourselves from it and its problems.

6. What is the difference between "carnal" and "spiritual" tools?

7. _____ received a special anointing to build the ark; _____ received one to run the Egyptian empire;

_____ received one to lead the people of Israel through the wilderness; _____ received several to take Jericho and the Promised Land; _____ received one to be the prime minister of Babylon; _____ received one to repair the wall. Each of these people operated at a level of supernatural efficiency made possible only by the _____ _____ _____ that was in them.

8. It is not enough to allow marketplace ministers to _____ in ministry. They need to become ministry _____. Furthermore, they should have a similar right to become _____. Ultimately, they must be welcome to _____.

B. Reflection and Discussion

1. Discuss your experience with deceit, incompetence, and spiritual deadlock and why these issues force a Christian into spiritual bankruptcy.

2. Many marketplace Christians face spiritual bankruptcy because they do not believe that they can hear God's voice at work. What are some of the benefits of hearing God's voice at work and some of the detriments of not hearing it?

3. With another person, read and pray through the first and second points of "A Spiritual Business Plan" on page 159.

C. My Journal

DOING BUSINESS GOD'S WAY

A. Study Guide

1. What is "anointing"?

2. If you know that God has anointed you for business, He will keep
_____ your sphere of influence until you
_____ the level He has chosen for you.

3. Only _____ are entrusted with the opportunity to move from "a few things" to "many things" simply because of their _____.

4. We do business God's way with the clear intent to see the marketplace _____.

5. Church is business—God's business, as Jesus called it—and that business can be _____ when church happens in the _____.

6. To be a successful marketplace Christian, you must recognize that you have been _____ and decide to
_____ The rest is entirely up to God.

B. Reflection and Discussion

1. Discuss a few examples of anointing in the Bible (David, Joseph, Esther, Priscilla and Aquila, Lydia, Naaman's little servant girl). Which is the most meaningful to you? Why?

2. Declare out loud in prayer with another person: I am anointed for business—God's Business. My job is my pulpit, and the marketplace is my parish. I have been called by God to bring His kingdom to the marketplace. I will go for it!

C. My Journal

Study Guide Answer Key

Introduction
1. business, education, government (p. 15)
2. parish, pulpit (p. 16)
3. transformation (p. 17-18)
4. See the "Four Lethal Misbeliefs" on pages 20-21.

Chapter 1
1. Full-time consecration to God and His work (p. 28)
2. Part-time (p. 28)
3. transform, environment (p. 29)
4. marketplace (p. 29)
5. entire world (p. 29)

Chapter 2
1. craftsmen (pp. 34-36)
2. To show God's heart for the marketplace; to get in touch with the heart of the city from the beginning of His earthly life (p. 34)
3. entrepreneur, leader, connoisseur, business (pp. 35-37)
4. calculation of the costs of goods and labor, the interplay between supply and demand, the establishment of competitive pricing, the measurement of the potential return on investment, the estimation of maintenance costs and replacement of equipment (p. 36)
5. See "Jesus the Marketplace Connoisseur" on pages 36-37.
6. The notion that Jesus was perpetually broke is not scriptural. He operated with great comfort in the marketplace and was known to have done honest work for a living (pp. 38-39).
7. Work, worship (p. 39)

Chapter 3
1. marketplace, marketplace (p. 42)
2. nonreligious, backbone, ministry, leaders, theological (pp. 43-46)

3. partner (p. 47)
4. Temple, outward, Persecution (p. 48)
5. Extraordinary results, specifically many conversions in the midst of dramatic power encounters (p. 49)
6. counterculture, subculture (p. 50)

Chapter 4

1. Old Testament, marketplace (p. 54)
2. spiritual, secular, central (p. 55)
3. profit motive, drive to win, boundaries, challenges (p. 56)
4. He saw God deeply interested in everything he did; his job was his ministry and his ministry was his job (p. 58).
5. material, spiritual (p. 58)
6. The devil is afraid that Christians will fulfill their divine destiny in the marketplace and bring the kingdom of God to it (p. 59).
7. By debasing their occupation, by telling them that it is less spiritual than Church work, and by painting them as materialistic and unspiritual (p. 59).

Chapter 5

1. God despises rich people; success is something that Christians cannot handle well (p. 65)
2. all, wealthy, destitute, both (p. 66)
3. marketplace, authority, success (p. 70)
4. authority over cities (p. 70)
5. identified (p. 73)
6. trust, liberally, bless, provider, replenisher (p. 75)

Chapter 6

1. ethnic, denominational, ministerial, gender, generational, marketplace (pp. 78-79)
2. lives, resources, believers, added, poor, evangelism (p. 82, 85)
3. hope, faith, love (p. 88)
4. proportionally (p. 90)

Chapter 7

1. transform, environment, conditions (p. 94)
2. yesterday, in the future, today (p. 95)
3. tangible, interpersonal relationships (p. 96)
4. building, taking (p. 97)
5. dynamic, expansive, confined, centripetal (p. 97)
6. bring the kingdom of God to Earth, empowered, commissioned (p. 99, 100)
7. men and women, masters and slaves, parents and children who have been set free from the kingdom of darkness and transferred to the Kingdom of light. These people carry that Kingdom with them wherever they go (p. 101).
8. marketplace, evangelistic (p. 102)
9. marketplace (pp. 102-103)

Chapter 8

1. light of the world, salt of the earth, heart of the city (p. 110)
2. copying, non-Christian (p. 113)
3. worshiping, labor, caring for God's creation (pp. 118-119)

Chapter 9

1. embrace, transform, power (p. 122)
2. Even though both groups loved Jesus, the Twelve also resented sinners (p. 123)
3. blessing, fellowship, care, proclamation (p. 124)
4. join the system, embrace it, improve it, and bring the kingdom of God to it (p. 124)
5. neutralize, blessings (p. 128)
6. miracle (p. 129)
7. Light, darkness (p. 135)

Chapter 10

1. Obedience, understanding (p. 138)
2. failures, victories (pp. 143-144)
3. Obedience, fear (p. 144)

4. grace, sin, grace (p. 145)

Chapter 11
1. meet God's standards (p. 148)
2. deceit, incompetence, deadlock (p. 149)
3. transparent, lose control, disciplined (p. 149)
4. death, serious, dangerous, lethal, love, provision, repentance (pp. 149-150)
5. Spirituality (p. 151)
6. Carnal tools rely simply upon human wisdom; spiritual tools are supernaturally empowered by God for you to minister in business His way (p. 152).
7. Noah, Joseph, Moses, Joshua, Daniel, Nehemiah, Spirit of God (pp. 152-153)
8. participate, peers, partners, lead (p. 157)

Chapter 12
1. God's empowerment to do His work so that the will of God will be done on Earth (p. 164).
2. expanding, reach (p. 165)
3. servants, faithfulness (p. 171)
4. transformed (p. 172)
5. church, marketplace (p. 174)
6. anointed for business, obey God and use that anointing (p. 174)

Section I
My Spiritual
Business Plan

A. Declaring Chapter 11

1. Dealing with sin (see pages 149-152)
   - Personal—ask the Lord if there is any personal sin that is hindering your anointing for business. Confess any sin God brings to mind and ask for His grace to turn away from it completely.
   - Corporate—ask the Lord if there is any corporate sin that is hindering your business. Confess any sin God brings to mind and ask for His grace to turn away from it completely.

2. Dedication of my workplace (see number 3 on page 160).
   Set a date to officially welcome the Lord Jesus into your workplace for His perfect efficiency to replace your own deficiency or insufficiency. (If you have done this already, do it again with renewed commitment to do business God's way.)

   - The date and time I will do this are _____.
   - I will invite _____ to pray with me (if applicable).
   - I will ask the Lord to help me walk with Him daily in my place of business, being aware of His presence and influence on my thoughts and actions.

3. Select a place at work as "my place to meet with God" (see number 4 on page 160). That place is _____
   _____
   _____
   _____.

4. Recognize the Trinity as the head of the corporation where you work. Acknowledge this through prayer (see number 5 on pages 160-161).

B. Finding My Destiny in the Marketplace

- I will focus on the lost and recognize that there is a plentiful harvest of people who need to be brought in. What "focusing on the lost" means for me practically is . . .

- I will accept the challenge not to shy away from the harvest field but to go deeper into it. What "going deeper into the harvest" means for me practically is . . .

- With God's help, I will deliberately follow the four steps in Luke 10 as applied to the marketplace:

1. Join the system by accepting it as God's starting point for you. Speak peace to it. Thank God for it.

   Application Action: I will begin to speak peace to my business and bless in prayer those who work with me _____ times per week. (This commitment can easily be fulfilled daily as you walk into and exit the office: "Father God, I speak peace to _____ Corporation. Bless _____ and reveal Yourself to them in a personal way.")

2. Embrace the system by giving everything you have to your current job and to those with whom you are working.

   Application Actions:
   - I will make a list of the good things my job has to offer and affirm them:

- As I speak peace to and bless those around me, I will also look for ways to improve and develop those relationships through God-led fellowship. One person I will seek out is _____ _____. One way I can relate to this person is _____ _____.

3. Improve the system by praying for the felt needs that exist in the business or in a person's life.

    Application Action: I will be observant and meet the felt needs of the business and those in my circle of influence. One felt need of the person I listed above is _____. I will begin to pray for this need. One way I can care for this person and his/her need (other than prayer) is _____ _____.

4. Bring the kingdom of God to my job because I am blessing my job, embracing it, and bringing peace as I pray for the felt needs of my coworkers.

    Application Actions:
    - As God draws near to those I am praying for, I will let them know that it is Jesus answering my prayers on their behalf, and share that God is drawing near to them because He loves them and wants them to know Him.

    - If I do not know how to share the gospel and lead someone to Jesus Christ, I will learn by _____ _____ (date and manner).

C. Describe the Process

Describe what the process might look like as the kingdom of God comes to your business (e.g., language improves, company morale increases, dishonesty decreases).

Section II
My Path to Marketplace Reconciliation

A. Choose a financial ceiling

- Establish a ceiling for how much money you wish to live on. Pick a figure that is comfortable—you can always reduce it.

- Once you have chosen a figure with which you feel comfortable, make a decision that every penny over that ceiling will be given to the needy (someone who has no possibility of repaying the gift or even thanking you properly).

B. Defeat poverty of the spirit by allowing the unbelieving world to see clearly that Christians of different social positions love each other. Reach out to Christians in your circle of influence who are at a lower financial or social standing than you. Two people God is leading me to contact are _____ and _____ .

1. Consciously and consistently plan to pray and worship with them. One way I can do this is _____ _____ .

2. Speak into his or her life and let him or her speak into yours. One way I can do this is _____ _____ .

C. Commit to marketplace transformation

1. What sins in the marketplace will I forsake?

    • *If I have played a role in the increase of these sins of the marketplace, I repent and ask God for His help to turn away from these sins. I will also ask that as the Lord forgives, He will heal and restore.*

2. What do I want to see increase in the marketplace (the opposite of what you are forsaking)?

    • *I will be a leader in seeing these actions increase in the marketplace. I will pray for God's grace and strength to act on what He has put into my heart.*

D. For Employers

1. Three things I can do to minister to my employees:

2. Two things I can do to enable my employees to live debt-free:

SECTION III
MY COMMITMENT
CALENDAR

A. I will reevaluate my commitments and review progress made on . . .

(Record dates)

_____ (1 month from today)

_____ (3 months from today)

_____ (6 months from today)

_____ (12 months from today)

B. My journal of progress and renewed commitment:

THANKS

Let me express my deepest gratitude to Steven Lawson, my editor when we began to work on this book and my friend by the time we reached the last chapter, and to Cindy Laube-Oliveira, my faithful assistant who improved a fluid manuscript with her God-given touch for perfection.

I also want to recognize the wonderful people at Regal Books who went many extra miles with me to get into print this message that has been burning in my heart. Thank you Bill Greig III, Kyle Duncan, Deena Davis, Kim Bangs, Nola Grunden and Elizabeth Wingate. I could not have completed this work without your vision, prayers and expertise.

OTHER BOOKS BY
ED SILVOSO

Women: God's Secret Weapon

God's Inspiring Message to Women of Power, Purpose and Destiny

Prayer Evangelism

How to Change the Spiritual Climate

over Your Home, Neighborhood and City

That None Should Perish

How to Reach Entire Cities for Christ Through Prayer Evangelism

Additional Works by Ed Silvoso

ANOINTED FOR BUSINESS Audio Book

This audio version of the book by the same title, read by Ed Silvoso himself, will make the perfect companion for your daily driving or home study time. Available in CD or Cassette!

WOMEN GOD'S SECRET WEAPON Study Guide

This study guide can be used with the Regal book that speaks to both women and men on the awesome role of women in God's kingdom. Ed Silvoso reveals how much God values women, and the most special role reserved for them in His master plan, including the delivery of the final blow to Satan's kingdom. Women and men will discover the keys for walking in the God-ordained partnership He always intended for them.

TRANSFORMATION IN THE MARKETPLACE DVD

This DVD presents four riveting true stories of how God is transforming a prison system, a city, a state and a continent, PLUS a step-by-step "how-to" teaching section by Ed Silvoso with powerful insights on how to apply it in your sphere of influence. Additional Transformation DVDs coming soon!

And for the family...

VICTORY AT HOME Audio Series

A dynamic, insightful four-tape series by Ed Silvoso designed to help couples rediscover intimacy and learn how to prepare children for adolescence with Kingdom values. Rich in biblical and practical insights, this is an ideal tool to restore families to God's intended fullness.

BECOMING AN OVERCOMER Audio Series

In this two-tape series, Ed Silvoso shows how to identify and dismantle spiritual strongholds. Ed defines a stronghold as a mindset impregnated with hopelessness that forces us to accept as unchangeable situations that we know are contrary to the will of God. A session on how to forgive the unforgivable is also included.

Visit the Harvest Evangelism website to acquire these and other titles, to learn about upcoming seminars in your area and Argentina training trips, and to access a variety of practical "how-to" tools by Ed Silvoso and the Harvest Evangelism team.

www.harvestevan.org
1.800.835.7979

HARVEST
EVANGELISM

P.O. Box 20310 • San Jose, CA 95160-0310

.